Selling to the Point has the potential
to forever transform the way you think
about buying and selling!

Change is in the air at Essentials, Inc. The company's survival is
at stake and difficult decisions lie ahead. Should they sell out to
investors and give up their ideals as an independent enterprise?
Or can they find a way to change from within and somehow
thrive? To make the company look good to investors, the first
person facing the axe is Rick, the company sales trainer, who's
known for his unorthodox style. But management begins to
take a closer look at Rick's techniques for improving salesperson
performance. They discover a treasure trove of insights, which
Rick calls "Selling To The Point". Can Rick's radical ideas be
the answer to Essential's dilemma? This unique business novel
digs deep into old, unquestioned assumptions in an unforgettable
way and reveals a new path for successful selling.

ABOUT THE AUTHOR

How did Jeffrey Lipsius develop his breakthrough
approach to selling? In fact, it is a culmination of
Jeffrey's passion for sales and his lifelong mission
to discover the key to peak performance. His
quest began on the tennis court at age nineteen.
He realized achieving tennis excellence required mental skills
as well as physical. His coaches, however, didn't have answers
to how tennis players could practice their mental state similarly
to practicing a forehand or backhand. Jeffrey's quest led him
to the disciplines of yoga and meditation. Then he came upon
a book called *The Inner Game of Tennis,* authored by Timothy
Gallwey. Gallwey's book made everything clear to Jeff about the
mental side of performance. By applying principles of The Inner
Game, he learned to access inner awareness and apply it during
matches. His performance transformed substantially both on
and off the court.

After college, Jeffrey began his lifelong career as a sales professional. While attending a conference, Jeffrey had the great fortune
to meet his tennis mentor Timothy Gallwey. They shared ideas
about applying The Inner Game to salesperson performance.
Jeffrey's new mission was born. He became a regular attendee at
Gallwey's workshops, which inspired him to creatively integrate
new insights and fine-tune his training. As he trained salespeople,

Jeffrey adapted The Inner Game's principles to improve their performance. This process continued for over twenty years.

Jeffrey achieved remarkable results with the unique training approach that emerged. He was his company's highest producer. He got promoted to vice president. He trained hundreds of other salespeople to be leading performers in their industries. Jeffrey is introducing this system for peak selling performance in this book. He calls it Selling To The Point®, and he is passionate about the changes you will experience by applying his method.

SELLING
TO THE POINT

SELLING
TO THE POINT

BECAUSE THE INFORMATION AGE
DEMANDS A NEW WAY TO SELL

A Story

JEFFREY LIPSIUS

RRP

Pacific Palisades, CA

Rydal Road Publishing
15332 Antioch St. Ste. 358
Pacific Palisades, CA 90272
(831)350-0148

First Edition

Printed in the United States of America

Names: Lipsius, Jeffrey, author.

Title: Selling to the point : because the information age demands a new way to sell : a story / Jeffrey Lipsius.

Description: First edition. | Pacific Palisades, CA : Rydal Road Publishing, [2015]

Identifiers: ISBN: 978-0-9964759-0-7 | LCCN: 2015908769

Subjects: LCSH: Selling. | Sales. | Sales management. | Sales personnel--Training of. | Sales force management. | Internet marketing. | Digital communications. | Electronic commerce. | Information society. | Purchasing. | Success in business.

Classification: LCC: HF5438.25 .S45 2015 | DDC: 658.85--dc23

Author Photo: Leslie Bohm
Interior Design and Layout: Ghislain Viau

This book is dedicated to my mother and father,
who introduced me to the selling profession; Sherri Kramer Saget,
who supported me throughout this book's creation; and Prem
Rawat, who put me in touch with the clarity I was looking for.

CONTENTS

ACKNOWLEDGMENTS

THIS BOOK WOULD NOT HAVE BEEN POSSIBLE WITHOUT THE wisdom of my two most influential mentors, Prem Rawat and Timothy Gallwey. Tim Gallwey, through his inner game method, showed me how to achieve performance beyond expectations. I'm deeply appreciative for the brilliant insights they so generously shared with me over many decades.

I'm grateful for all the support I received from Sherri Kramer Saget, including her contributions to the creative and logistical processes required for writing *Selling To The Point*.

I want to thank all the teachers and trainers whose ideas formed many of *Selling To The Point*'s principles. The teachings of Dr. Stephen Wolinsky, the late James South, Mark Victor Hansen, Jon Kabat Zinn, Fred Kofman, and Peter Senge all contributed to my understanding of how people interact in the workplace.

A special thanks goes to Gerald Sindell and Sherri Kramer Saget for collaborating with me on writing the book itself.

Last but not least, I want to thank all the salespeople I coached who agreed to let me practice my theories on them. It was their patience and adventurous spirit that made this book possible.

FOREWORD
by Timothy Gallwey

JEFF LIPSIUS HAS WRITTEN ONE HELLUVA BOOK FOR PEOPLE who sell and buy. This book is not just another stale method on how to exceed your sales quota. Jeff's message is quite unique, emphasizing a seemingly obvious but often unconscious mindset. "Selling is not the point of the conversation," he proclaims. "Buying is the point. And the key process involved in buying is the buying decision that can only be made by the buyer." As a professional sales trainer, Mr. Lipsius saw the tremendous implications of this perspective on the role of the salesperson and how he or she could best be trained.

The more traditional method of selling, Jeff says, *interferes* more than we may expect with the buyer's ability to use his or her best resources while making the buying decision. Even if the deal is made, the buyer may remember the seller's reasons for the purchase over his own. The simple fact that the exchange has occurred does not necessarily guarantee that the buyer will make good use of the product, or come back for more.

Not long after the publication of *The Inner Game of Tennis*, I began having conversations with Jeff Lipsius while he was still a manager and lead sales trainer in a successful enterprise in the health supplement industry. The main thing I had learned from playing and teaching tennis was just how much traditional instruction invited mental interference with the natural learning process within the player. It could, in fact, not only slow down the learner's rate of skill development, but also generate cycles of self-doubt, self-judgment, and an over-dependency on instructions that could impair power, accuracy, and motivation for years.

One day I mentioned to Jeff that I saw a similar pattern in salesmanship. I asked something I'd always been curious about: "Why, in the interaction between a buyer and a seller, is the conversation called 'selling'? And why would buyers agree to this obviously one-sided definition? Which is more important to both parties—the selling process or the buying process?"

To Jeff's great credit, he took this simple paradoxical observation and examined its impact on how selling is trained and delivered—and perhaps more importantly, its impact on the decision process of the buyer. From this exploration, a new way for salespeople to see their role from an entirely different perspective emerged, turning an archaic set of selling tactics into a natural process to help buyers make better decisions. And what happens? As buyers realize the salesperson is on their team, the all-too-familiar resistance to being pressured evaporates. A new level of trust emerges between buyer and seller that frees the buyer to think for him or herself while the salesperson becomes more of a decision *coach*.

As you might imagine, the concept of learning a sport without needing to be taught the do's and don'ts was not overwhelmingly supported by the tennis pros who considered it their job to teach all the rights and wrongs of proper technique they had once learned from their instructor. It was this kind of knowledge that most tennis teachers considered the value they had to pass on to those who didn't yet have the proper know-how. "That's what I get paid for," exclaimed one instructor. "Without doing that, where is my value?"

My answer to this is, "Technique in itself is obviously important. But what if there is a better way to learn technique than being told in words?" The value is in the learning, not in the telling. When the student is coached to learn any technique by paying attention to how it feels and how it works, by observation without trying to consciously manipulate the stroke, the tennis student is learning how to learn from experience. *While* learning tennis, you are learning how to learn most anything.

Selling To The Point anticipates this scenario, giving voice to those who cling to the adage of the prevalent schools of sales training, which assert that the salesperson who controls the selling conversation will earn the most commission. Which approach will win? Sell by trying to take control, or sell by facilitating the buying process of each buyer? There are many selling/buying situations, from retail sales to long-term relationship selling. My bet favors that *Selling To The Point* will win, both for the salesperson and for the buyer. Both will increase their learning and a relationship of trust will grow. This delivers ongoing value to both parties in almost any kind of communication.

Some may be thinking that sales management may not be very supportive of such an outcome. Not true. Any manager who embraced *Selling To The Point* would realize three things:

1. Salespeople experience accelerated learning, whether the customer buys or not. *Selling To The Point* means salespeople have greater awareness of their customers' needs and decision processes, giving both buyer and seller greater probabilities for success. And with this approach, salespeople will be more amenable to having discussions with their managers about how their customers' decision making could improve. This is in sharp contrast with how most conversations today are being conducted at sales meetings. In today's workplace, managers think their job is to highlight their salespeople's shortcomings, to give feedback (should and shouldn'ts), which generally only raises salespeople's resistance, conscious or unconscious.

2. Greater customer awareness allows salespeople to be more accurate when reporting back to their company about how product presentations are being received. This information empowers companies to make the necessary modifications for attaining desired performance goals.

3. When salespeople genuinely support their buyer's decision making, a foundation of trust establishes itself. This trust emerges naturally. The need for salespeople to over-control

to establish their goals is avoided. The recognition that the salesperson sincerely wants the best decision to be made naturally develops the trust and loyalty toward his or her salesperson—a result that is priceless.

What is equally brilliant about this book is how readable it has been made by virtue of the author's choice to write it in the form of fiction. *Selling To The Point*'s principles and methods can be learned effortlessly by simply following the story and its dialogues between the various characters. This allows the reader to examine both the pros and cons of the methodology and to arrive at his or her own decision about its efficacy, quite in the same manner as the author recommends the buyer is left free to think for him or herself.

I believe that many salespeople will see the wisdom of experimenting with Lipsius's approach to see how it feels, how it affects their relationship with the buyer, and, of course, how it affects sales productivity in the long run.

I predict that with a little practice and perhaps some training, it will become the prevailing approach in the buying-selling conversation simply because it makes both economic and human sense.

This book is among the best applications of the inner game style of thinking that I have read. Although this book is not an official Inner Game book, Jeff has created a brilliant application that combines his understanding of the inner game with his expertise in sales in a unique and practical way. I would argue that this approach has much greater integrity than that of others who have used the Inner Game brand because of their lack of the effort necessary for understanding the essence of the meaning behind it.

He may have come up with the most influential book for sales in a decade. If so, his publishers will be very happy and perhaps a bit surprised. My own editor of the *The Inner Game of Tennis* predicted in 1974 that based on the tennis market, a reasonable sales target for the book was in the vicinity of twenty thousand copies sold. When the sales had climbed to over a million copies, and became the best selling book in the field of tennis and sports psychology, I asked my editor how he would explain being so wrong with his original estimate. His reply was the following: "Well, we didn't expect that the majority of readers would not be tennis players. The book was bought by people who saw a better way to learn anything, including it as required reading in a leading university course in advance structural engineering, and by a student of a renowned violinist who said it was the best book ever written on playing the violin."

Buyers will benefit from the uniqueness of this inner game book in many ways. I like that! They will reclaim their decisiveness and agency as the key to the entire process. Where necessary, they will take back a bit of lost control, be more open about their needs, and arrive at better buying decisions.

"Selling" is not just a commercial activity of exchanging products or services for money. Leaders "sell" ideas and too easily fall into manipulation. Classroom teachers who "sell" their lessons to the young buyers in those rows of chairs might find more motivation and benefit if their teachers were more like coaches of the students' process of understanding. The teacher may have the authority to teach granted by degree and school, but the students undeniably have the final control and in fact the authority, just like the buyer, to buy or not buy what is being offered by the teacher.

For relationships between parents and children, between romantic partners, and between citizens and their governments, the applications of Lipsius's approach are innumerable. The principle is simple: Let the people who actually have the control of a particular decision exercise that control. And let the helpers learn from the learners from which they will gain greater control over how they connect with others authentically.

In general, one's inner game is the responsibility of each individual. For each to accept that authority is the essence of being conscious: making choices on the basis of one's own understanding of any given situation, and benefiting from what works and what doesn't work.

I hope all serious readers of this book understand that how they develop their understanding of their inner game and how they apply it are their decisions. The consequences will follow the natural laws of selection of the best ways to decide for ourselves, and there will be a continual development in how we communicate with each other. Who knows? We might even learn to recognize ways to resolve conflict within ourselves then help others do the same, and in the end contribute toward a more peaceful world.

INTRODUCTION

I LOVE SELLING. I LOVE BEING PART OF THE SELLING PROFES-
sion. During my forty-year career, I've been involved in every
role: salesperson, sales manager, sales trainer, and vice president
of sales. My favorite of all is introducing someone to the selling
profession and training him or her to be successful. Fortunately,
I have many success stories.

Over the years, I noticed the best results happened when I
trained a new salesperson myself. Although I've been to many
sales seminars and read many sales training books, I was never
comfortable trusting traditional sales training methods to indoc-
trinate my recruits. I have come to understand that traditional
sales training misses the point of selling.

Although I did not set out in life to become an author, the
time finally came that I could no longer sit by and watch sales
trainers lead new salespeople down a path from which they might
never recover. I decided it was time to step in and simply write
what I know to be true from my own years of experience. I'm

1

doing this now because the selling profession, one that I care so much about, is being threatened like never before. The Internet allows potential customers to buy virtually anything without consulting salespeople. If the way salespeople are trained doesn't catch up with how customers are now buying, selling as a profession will falter. Some companies have already replaced their sales staff with ecommerce systems. When I hear TV commercials offer as a perk, "No salesperson will call you," I know the way salespeople are being trained needs a reboot.

Why do I care so much about the profession of selling? Because salespeople can move the world. They introduce valuable new ideas to a world that often would prefer to stand still rather than be part of progress. Salespeople are the lifeblood of the marketplaces of ideas. Without them, the world would continue to turn, but the adoption of better ideas would be slowed.

Why aren't salespeople generally valued for the genuine contributions they make? Potential customers tend to avoid them because of the way salespeople are traditionally trained. They are trained to be self-conscious. They're given scripts and selling points to present. Then they're sent into the field expecting customers to conform to their needs. And of course, this is absurd! Customers shouldn't be concerned with what salespeople expect of them. Customers should simply be busy trying to decide if they should buy or not.

Selling To The Point introduces a new approach to selling. It starts by showing salespeople how to be conscious instead of self-conscious. It will explain the principles, mind-set, and techniques necessary to influence customers at the point of their decision process. Traditional sales training refers to the customer's decision process as the "black box"; in this book, we will unlock that black box.

The first step is for salespeople to speak their customer's language. In order to walk my talk, I teach my approach in a story format, rather than as an instruction manual. The richest source of information for salespeople comes from their dialogue with customers. As the story unfolds, you will learn the principles of Selling To The Point through the language of dialogue, which is the language of sales. You'll be able to learn a new method of selling at the only place and time that it counts: at the point of interaction between salesperson and customer.

You don't have to be a salesperson to derive value from *Selling To The Point*. It will be immediately useful for anyone who wants to more effectively influence the decision making of others.

Selling To The Point is not just about selling. It's about a basic life skill that helps us understand both how the world works and how to find a fulfilling path in that world.

Chapter 1

NO ONE'S PAYING YOU TO SELL
The Point of Selling

LAW #1:

**SALESPEOPLE WILL BE MORE SUCCESSFUL
WHEN THEY UNDERSTAND THAT THE
POINT OF SELLING ISN'T SELLING. THE
POINT OF SELLING IS BUYING.**

MARTIN SAMUELS HEADED OUT THE DOOR OF HIS CONDO TO begin another week as CFO of Essentials, Inc. After his divorce, Essentials had become more than his work—it was his oasis, the one place he could find order and predictability. Work was pretty much the opposite of what home was these days. At home, he certainly didn't expect to find order and predictability as he attempted to do a decent job of co-parenting his fifteen-year-old daughter, Fiona.

Martin noticed a cool breeze stirring. Autumn was in the air, and it suddenly hit him that he'd been so preoccupied at

Essentials that he hadn't quite noticed that summer was almost gone. End of the girls' softball league season. Maybe the last year for him to coach his daughter's team.

Martin swung his Lexus into the Essentials parking lot, grabbed his computer, and headed inside, greeting everyone by name as he headed to his office. The first message in Martin's inbox was from Joan, the CEO. She was asking for a quick meeting this morning to kick off the investor reporting project. Damn! The board had green-lighted the sale of some shares to outside investors. It meant that in spite of Martin's projections, the board believed that Essentials, an excellent but midmarket wholesaler of medical supplies, was no longer adequately capitalized to remain competitive.

Strangely enough, one could blame social media for putting pressure on a company such as Essentials. The fear that any cutback in service quality would immediately be screamed all over the web meant that nothing could be done that would risk triggering a rise in complaints. Joan and the board were in a defensive crouch.

The board's decision to move ahead with the outside investor project didn't come as a complete surprise. While he knew it was a good, conservative business decision under the circumstances, Martin was hoping against hope that Essentials would continue to be his oasis. Now he feared today would be the beginning of that changing as well.

Martin stepped into Joan's office with a light knock on the door. There was no need for formalities—they'd been through a lot together at Essentials. Each of them had a pretty good idea what the other was doing at just about any point in time. Martin sat down in his regular chair and waited for Joan to finish what she was doing.

Joan had the appearance of someone who preferred to stand out. A tall redhead in her late forties, she looked every inch the leader in her confident, colorful suits. Martin had often witnessed how easily she could make new people feel comfortable in her presence, with a personality both bubbly and affable. Yet Martin also knew the other Joan—all business and bottom line—and she could switch with stunning speed.

Joan didn't waste time with any greetings. "We're going ahead with outside investors, so I need you to start getting reports together, and they need to be good. I'm especially concerned about the sales department report because profits are in the tank in spite of strong sales. Damn the price of fuel—we thought it would be cheap forever!"

Martin was taking notes. "Time frame?"

"I'm meeting with the board tonight. We'll obviously need to reduce salespeople's travel to only core metropolitan areas. It costs too much for them to continue visiting the 'burbs and beyond. I think we have to accept that calling on those customers just requires greater travel distances than we can afford. And please scan through sales department expenses today. Let me know if you see anything else we can cut. I'd like to bring the board as much as possible to get things on a positive footing.

"Can you work your magic and put together a decent-looking projected balance sheet for sales?"

"No problem, Joan," Martin quickly replied. "I'll give you a call by four."

Joan's comment about Martin "working magic" had stroked his ego. The only problem was that by taking the bait, he would need to come up with sales department cost cuts virtually on the fly.

Cutting back on travel was a no-brainer, except that there was less competition in the lower-density regions because competing salespeople didn't visit them as much. But there was also a structural opportunity. Essentials had a fairly archaic structure in which different Essentials salespeople might be covering the same territory, just with different products from different vendors. Maybe the time had come to assign salespeople by area rather than by product line.

Over the past few years, Martin hadn't really been paying close attention to the sales department, relying instead on the sales manager, Ben. Ben seemed to be running a tight ship, but now Martin was beginning to get a nagging feeling that his *laissez-faire* approach to sales might be about to come back and bite him somewhere tender.

As soon as Martin got back to his office, he brought up the sales department expense register. It didn't take long to notice a substantial item for a sales trainer position—some guy named Rick. He spun back through the records. Holy Toledo! The guy had been training there for fourteen years. Should've gotten it right by now. A big "Aha" went through Martin's head. Rick could be the lowest-hanging-fruit, the cost-cutting opportunity he was looking for.

Martin instantly picked up the phone to leave Joan a voice-mail. He said, "Joan, I found the first savings. Sales has a trainer on the payroll whom we probably don't need. The department's too small to support one, especially at his pay level. I'll do more investigating, but consider this your answer. And it's five hours earlier than promised."

Martin knew the process of laying off a fourteen-year veteran would need to be handled delicately. He would need to bring Ben around to his side. He picked up the phone and asked Ben to arrange a meeting with Rick without telling him the purpose. Ben, for some unknown reason, seemed surprisingly eager to help Martin and Rick get together. The meeting was set for the next morning.

Rick arrived at Martin's office right on time. Rick wasn't the kind of guy you'd notice in a crowd any larger than two people. In his early fifties, he was short and slight with a wispy shock of gray hair arranged in an unsuccessful comb-over.

Martin began the meeting by explaining to Rick that Essentials was starting the process of seeking outside investment. Among those responsibilities would be reviewing financial projections for every department, and he wanted Rick's input.

Martin continued, "So your training style has been described as somewhat unconventional. What does that mean?"

Rick took the bait. He loved talking about his training philosophy. "The two people in my life who influenced how I train salespeople were my father and my autistic nephew, Jace. I have Jace to thank for giving me the key insight on which I have based my entire training. And here it is: The first law of selling—the point of selling isn't selling; the point of selling is buying."

Rick paused there to let the brilliance of his insight sink in. As a skilled observer, he suspected it hadn't. Nevertheless, he waited, forcing Martin to go first.

"Huh. That sounds interesting, but what does it mean? And how could you learn that from an autistic nephew?"

Rick smiled approvingly at the aptness of Martin's question. "Makes one wonder, doesn't it? You see, by the time Jace had become a teenager, I noticed he made very accurate yet highly unusual observations, which I would look forward to when I had the chance to see him. And although I thought he was often full of insight, I was really surprised to see how many people around Jace ignored him.

"For instance, one day, when Jace was filling up a glass of water to drink, I asked him, 'Hey, Jace, what are you up to?' And he replied, 'I'm noticing the distance between the water level and the top of the glass.'

"And I thought, 'Whoa!' Jace was describing what we all do when we fill up a glass with water, but most of us don't have the awareness to realize what's actually going on. On another occasion my sister, Jace's mom, said to him, 'How come you're just sitting around doing nothing?' And Jace replied, 'But I'm not doing nothing. My heart is beating, I'm breathing, I'm digesting. I'm…' And he would have continued reciting the list of his metabolic processes if she hadn't stopped him.

"His way of seeing the world was contagious. Later that day, I was watching a hummingbird. I noticed how much activity the hummingbird required to appear still. I realized I was beginning to think like Jace."

Martin was not all that introspective, and Rick's digressions were beginning to annoy him. "It's very nice that you value your autistic nephew's observations, but would you please tell me what the heck this has to do with sales training?"

Rick was unflappable. "Okay, look at this. Once during a visit, Jace asked me what I do for work. I answered that I'm a salesman. I described to him what salespeople do, in the kind of detail he appreciated. When I finished, Jace announced, 'Then I don't understand why the job is called selling when your money is made from customers buying. Why do you care about selling when you're just paid for buying?'"

Martin was not overwhelmed by the insight. "Seems like the same thing to me."

Rick replied, "I felt the same way as you do, at first. The next day, however, the wisdom of Jace's observation became clear. I was accompanying a new saleswoman, Doreen, on an appointment. She and I spent that morning rehearsing selling points. We felt amply prepared for anything the client might say. Ironically, the first thing that client said to us was the one thing we weren't prepared for. The client said, 'I thought about your product and decided to go ahead and buy it. Whom should I make the check out to?' Doreen looked surprised and began going over the selling points we had just rehearsed. Remembering Jace's wise words, I quickly interrupted by saying to the customer, 'Thank you very much. You can make the check out to Essentials, Inc.' We left the appointment shortly thereafter.

"The first time I found myself quoting the first law of selling—'The point of selling isn't selling; it's buying'—was to Doreen on our way back to the office. Jace's insight provided me with the perspective for giving salespeople a clear and simple goal. I explained to Doreen that the point of selling is buying. The customer had already bought, so selling to him would have been beside the point."

Rick went on, "As I got clearer about Jace's comment, everything fell into place. I began to recall instances when I had observed selling directly interfere with buying. I'd had a recent instance when a customer was ready to buy but changed her mind because the salesperson kept talking. I thought about how salespeople can try to make products sound complicated, which has resulted in customers becoming too confused to buy. I recalled customers losing interest because the salesperson exceeded the customers' attention span. Jace's insights eventually triggered a completely new understanding of how I view the profession of selling."

"So it's an interesting theory," Martin said, "but how does that change anything in the real world?"

Rick was quick to respond. "That's where my dad comes in. Dad's a farmer. He explained to me that people and plants share common qualities because they're both from nature. Dad would say farmers don't have to know about photosynthesis to reap a good harvest. They just need to support the process with water, soil, and sunlight. Mother Nature will do the rest.

"Now, thanks to Jace, I could see what Dad meant," Rick continued. "Salespeople don't need to figure out and control their customers' buying decisions. They're better off providing their customers' decision making with the support it needs. People enjoy buying. They don't enjoy being sold to. This is because buying and decision making—similar to a well-nourished plant—are natural. I train salespeople to cultivate sales the same way farmers grow crops."

Martin pondered that for a moment. "Crops! That's a new one. How does that translate into reality at Essentials?"

Rick said, "Take a look at this report that just came in this morning."

Martin flipped open the folder and read out loud, "Ravi made his buying decision for our sutures once I made him aware that low-quality sutures can dissolve prematurely."

Rick offered, "Here's another. I noticed Graciela, the purchaser, looked uncomfortable asking me questions about the new syringes I was presenting. I also noticed her manager was in the next cubicle and could hear everything we were saying. It seemed apparent to me that she felt self-conscious about asking me questions with him within earshot. She must not have wanted to reveal to him what parts of my presentation she didn't understand. I offered to continue the presentation off-site. She was a different person once we were away from the office. She was fully engaged this time. She kept asking questions until she was satisfied she knew enough about the syringes. Graciela placed a nice order. If anyone is planning on presenting a new product to Graciela, I recommend doing it outside of the office."

Rick handed Martin another report and said, "Here's what a typical report looked like before our people began to get it."

Martin read, "I presented our new stethoscope line to Anup and left him with samples."

Rick remarked, "Look at the difference. The information on those summaries is more valuable when salespeople focus on what their customer is doing instead of on what the salesperson did."

He had more. "We're also suddenly benefitting from that new distributor rating blog. The number one complaint about salespeople is that they're too pushy. And now there's starting to be a buzz about how easy it is to work with Essentials salespeople."

Rick could see that Martin was glazing over, so he took the initiative to wrap up the meeting. "Look, I can see you have a lot on your plate. Here's a little card with my first three laws written down. I made them so I can share the laws with our sales force."

Rick handed the 3X5 card to Martin, whose first reaction was to shrink back a little bit. Rick pulled the card back, as if Martin were a fish he hadn't quite hooked.

"You don't have to take it."

Martin smiled. "No, it's okay. Sometimes I get stuff better when someone tells it to me."

Rick handed him the card again, gave a slight bow, turned on his heel, and left Martin gazing at the card.

Martin read the card out loud.

> ## LAW #1:
>
> ### THE POINT OF SELLING IS BUYING.
>
> ## LAW #2:
>
> ### THE SALESPERSON'S JOB IS TO HELP CUSTOMERS MAKE BETTER BUYING DECISIONS.
>
> ## LAW #3:
>
> ### DECISION MAKING IS AN INTERNAL PROCESS FOR THE CUSTOMER.

That was a lot for Martin to think through on his own. "I think it will take Rick in person to explain how these laws translate into sales."

Chapter 2

HOW TO FIND THE WORLD'S BEST CUSTOMERS
Traditional Sales Training Misses the Point

MARTIN WAS HAVING A HARD TIME. HE HAD COMMITTED TO cutting Rick's salary to improve the sales department's bottom line—but he hadn't yet found justification for letting go of a popular, fourteen-year company veteran. What was really getting to him was that he couldn't understand how Rick trained salespeople without telling them what to do.

If Martin wanted to keep Rick, he would have the daunting task of justifying Rick to the board. Conversely, to dump Rick, he needed to be able to bring down Rick's value in the eyes of others.

Martin checked for messages from Joan in his inbox, praying he had more time. Good! Nothing from her yet. Next up, a meeting with Ben, Rick's boss. This was going to be tricky for Martin because he didn't want Ben to catch on to his plans.

Martin arrived at Ben's office early; Ben was already there, a whirlwind of energy, sorting the stack of papers in his arms into various piles on his desk. Aside from Ben's silver hair, the man was a poster child for the notion that sixty could be the new forty. As soon as Ben saw Martin, he greeted him with a two-handed handshake that took the place of the bear hug he really would have preferred to offer. But Essentials wasn't that much of a touchy-feely culture.

Martin began by asking if Ben was aware of the upcoming offer of Essentials shares to outside investors.

He was. "Actually, I'm glad the board decided to find more capital rather than slash costs. Cost cutting would have hurt our great service record, and that's not a path we want to go down."

Martin ignored the comment and continued talking. "So my first job in all of this is to generate financial reports from each department for investors to review. I'm starting with sales, and I want to be able to demonstrate that we're at or above industry benchmarks. For sales, it's all about continuing to grow sales while costs continue to get hammered down, down, down. And it's been a while since you and I crunched your numbers."

Ben replied, "It has been quite a while."

"That's because your department has performed so consistently well over the years that I left well enough alone. But now the sharp energy price jump has shuffled the deck. I think there's no question we've got to reduce salespeople's travel."

Ben was taken aback by the absoluteness of the statement. "Oh…"

"Sorry, but we can only afford to have them visit customers in the dense metro areas. Suburbia and beyond is just not going to work."

Ben began to absorb the impact of this new plan on everything he did. "Hmmm. When does this happen?"

Martin replied, "I don't want to do the incremental pain thing. I think we should introduce a complete program involving everything we decide on, do it once, and do it right."

"I guess if we have to…"

Martin kept rolling. "But before I delve into your department in detail, I thought I'd ask if you can think of any other changes that would kick performance up and get some easy target expenses outta here."

Ben was cautious. "Gee, Martin. I think of myself as someone who keeps things about as skinny as they can be all the time. Can I take some time to think about it and maybe come up with a list?"

Martin's left eyebrow formed a sudden arch. "Time? Sure, take some time; get it right. Can you get something to me by tomorrow?"

"I'm on it," Ben responded.

Martin made his move. "And while you're at it, include something about Rick."

"Rick?"

"Your trainer."

Ben thought about Rick, and it made him happy. "That's a good thought. Bringing Rick into the picture would certainly buff up our image for the investors."

Not what Martin wanted to hear. Shifting gears, he prodded Ben with a seemingly innocuous query: "Aren't you concerned that our investors may not fully appreciate Rick? He's sort of an odd duck for people who don't get what he's doing."

Ben thought about that. "Well, I guess you could see it that way."

Martin made his move. "So have you compiled data that would show Rick's ROI? That's what everyone's going to want."

Ben was not a huge fan of boiling everything down to one bottom line. "Of course I have sales comparisons over the years. What's really hard to measure are all the things that could've happened if we hadn't built our great customer relations that get us through product recalls, customer budget cuts, and gas shortages." He was careful not to overreact. "But I'll get you what you need."

Then Ben had a bright idea. "Martin, you have a few more minutes?"

Martin did, so Ben took him by the arm and marched him down the long hall to the salesroom bullpen. Most of the salespeople were out visiting customers, but a few were at their desks doing paperwork and making follow-up calls.

Ben brought Martin to a cubicle occupied by a bright-eyed saleswoman, Allison, who was just wrapping up a call.

"I'll get those research pieces to you within the hour," she said, and she hung up.

Ben made the introductions and then said, "Allison, you've been here only a few months, so you can probably remember how you thought about selling before you came across Rick."

Allison rolled her eyes at the thought of how things used to be. "It was a different world, no question."

"Before Essentials, what did you think your job was?" Ben asked.

Allison thought for a split second. "Control. We were drilled on a million different ways to control any sales conversation, from beginning to end. We were taught how to get the customer to start saying 'yes' to a bunch of small things, like isn't the weather nice? And then we'd move those yesses up the ladder."

Martin wondered, "So how well did it work?"

Allison gave a funny frown. "Sometimes okay, sometimes not. But it was always a power struggle. And the reality was that we couldn't even begin to control the most important conversation—the one between our buyer's ears. Basically, if the buyer started thinking, we were in trouble."

Martin was puzzled. "So tell me how Rick gets you to have more leverage on your customers' thinking."

Allison could see that Martin was pretty clueless about Rick's way. "Well, trying to control your customers' thinking is a side agenda promoted by traditional sales training, and it misses the point. In the end, it doesn't matter whether the purchase resulted from the salesperson's influence or if the customers decided to purchase on their own. At the end of the day, a sale is a sale."

Allison continued, "See, I used to get caught up in all the side agendas that traditional sales training mistakes for objectives. I could even believe I had done a great job even if my customer didn't buy. I'd watch my colleagues steam right through their pitch, determined to get it all in, even if the customer had tried unsuccessfully to get a word in edgewise."

Martin was skeptical. "Not to play the devil's advocate, but I know how salespeople think. They feel a sense of accomplishment when their influence leads to the sale. It just couldn't feel as rewarding if a salesperson just stood around until customers decided on their own to buy."

Suddenly a head popped up from an adjoining cubicle. "Hi, I'm Shahrokh. I couldn't help but jump in. Salespeople in need of ego gratification won't find it in Rick's approach. Salespeople who need to take credit for the result will be missing the point."

Martin: "So what's your reward?"

Shahrokh didn't need to think too long about that. "My commission check."

Allison agreed. "When I used to take credit for getting a sale, I was setting myself up to take the blame for losing sales. And when I'd have a few misses and rejections right in a row, I would begin to believe that I stunk and that maybe sales wasn't for me after all. And when you feel like a loser, it shows in every sales call. Your customers can read how you feel about yourself, and before you realize what's happening, you've created a vicious cycle."

That triggered something for Ben. "That spiral could be pretty contagious. When it got really bad at companies before Essentials, I was forced to bring in expensive motivational speakers, consultants, and weekend event planners, all in an attempt to break the cycle. The motivational speakers assure their own job security. They persuade salespeople to think they're great and that they can make customers buy. If some customers don't buy, the salespeople no longer believe they're so great. Once again, I'd need to bring in a motivational speaker. Now there's a number for you, Martin: tens of thousands not spent patching up a broken sales force."

Instead of taking comfort, Martin was actually beginning to get worried. "Look, describing Rick's approach to investors is going to sound as if we train salespeople to not try."

Ben replied, "Now that you mention it, trying is another side agenda."

Martin reacted with sarcasm. "Why am I not surprised you said that?"

Ben: "I'm serious," Ben insisted. "You tell me. Would you rather have a salesperson come back without a sale but honestly say he or she tried, or show up with the sale and say he or she didn't even have to try? If salespeople and sales management are true to the goal of buying, then measuring how hard salespeople try is beside the point."

Allison added, "Really. If I see a salesperson trying hard to sell me something, the first thing I wonder is why he or she is trying so hard. I think to myself, 'If this product is really so good for me, then why doesn't the salesperson relax and let me arrive at that conclusion for myself?' If I see that the salesperson is relaxed, that tells me it's probably a great product."

Ben turned to Shahrokh. "Shahrokh—do you have a sales summary handy?"

He did, and Ben asked him to read from it.

"This is about my customer at a large medical group," Shahrokh explained. "I wrote: Buyer is a recent transfer from a much larger care facility, so he was having a hard time getting his hands around having to buy such a wide range of supplies. I scouted some competitors of his of similar size and gave my new guy some anonymous examples of how the others organized their buying—how many vendors they were comfortable managing, how they made reordering as routine as possible, how they knew they were getting the best prices all the time.

"I basically laid several options out in front of him. He chose from each one the elements he liked best. Once he assembled an organized system, it was much easier for me to suggest how Essentials fits into his program."

Shahrokh looked up from his notes. "Not surprisingly, within a month or so, he became one of my best and easiest accounts. Thanks to my contribution, he makes high-quality buying decisions every day."

LAW #4:

THE CUSTOMER'S DECISION-MAKING PERFORMANCE IS MORE IMPORTANT THAN THE SALESPERSON'S SELLING PERFORMANCE.

At this point, Martin had heard enough. He could see that Ben was completely unmovable about Rick having a permanent place in Essentials.

He politely said, "Well, Ben, this meeting has been very enlightening. I'm learning more about Rick this week than I've learned in all the years I've been here. I'll think about our conversation and let you know if there's any more information I need. In the meantime, it would be great if you can prepare that list of suggested changes to help your department's balance sheet."

Martin thanked everyone and headed off down the hall. He muttered to himself, "How the hell do you fire Yoda?"

Chapter 3

IT'S NOT ABOUT THE SPLINT
Clarifying Selling Success

THE CONVERSATION WITH BEN HAD SHOWN MARTIN JUST
how much Rick had charmed everyone in the sales department,
but Martin regretted having let the sales department run on its
own without some kind of audit. Rick had clearly become woven
into the very fabric of that department. Martin wondered how
that could have happened without him even noticing the guy.

Martin decided his next step should be to discover what Rick
was currently doing. He found Rick's training schedule. "Aha!"
Martin said to himself. Rick had just been working yesterday
with a new salesperson, Sally. Martin phoned Ben, hoping he
could see Sally immediately, while Sally's memory of Rick's
training was still fresh.

Ben thought Sally would make a good candidate for Martin
to learn more about Rick's innovative approach because Sally
didn't have preconceived ideas about Rick. But Ben was reluctant

to ask his salespeople to drop what they were doing for a meeting. Sally hadn't been thrilled a couple of days ago when he told her the company's sales trainer would be riding along.

Sally had responded, "What for? I'm doing great. It's my first month here, and you said I was off to the best new start of anyone in the department."

Ben, in his easy, supportive manner, had replied, "Yes, Sally, you're off to a great start. But I have all new salespeople train with my trainer, Rick, no matter how experienced they are or how well they're doing. Please give Rick a chance—he's not your typical sales trainer."

Sally had pushed down her pride to look like a team player. She had been a salesperson all her life. The product she was selling for Essentials was Bactogone, a splint and tape combination used at hospitals and medical centers. The splints were bacteria-resistant and comfortable but more expensive than competitive brands. The theory was that the extra expense would pay for itself because the product would prevent costly infections. But to stay sterile, the splints required a special sterile tape. The sterile tape was also more expensive than regular medical tape. The manufacturer, Essential's vendor, hardly made money on the splints—its profit came from subsequent orders of the special sterile tape. Sally also didn't make much commission on the splint—though her commissions on tape sales would accumulate nicely if customers continued to order it.

The next day, Rick knocked on Sally's office door to let her know he had arrived for her training. When Rick entered, he was confronted by an imposing figure. Sally was almost six feet tall, blond-haired, and in her early thirties. She projected an aura of assertive self-confidence as she towered over Rick. Rick could read that she wasn't thrilled about the prospect of being trained by him, but he wasn't fazed. He was used to it.

Sally took Rick on what she thought would be an easy call, a hospital close to her home that had recently employed a new purchaser, Meg. Sally took pride in her "new girl pitch," which involved getting the sale from a new purchaser by convincing him or her that the previous purchaser had been about to place an order but ran out of time before leaving. She felt this scenario provided the highest chance of closing a sale with Rick watching, assuring a good report to Ben. With that, Rick would be off her back.

As Rick and Sally drove to the appointment, Rick asked about her previous selling experience. Sally described to Rick her career salesperson background and how she loved the profession. She even came from a family of salespeople. When she was growing up, she always won the best prizes for wrapping-paper drives. She told Rick that she still loved learning new selling techniques and was a ravenous consumer of books on selling.

Rick and Sally arrived at the hospital, where Sally wasted no time navigating to the purchasing department and introducing herself to Meg. Meg was much younger than the previous purchaser and seemed nervous about her new responsibilities.

Sally explained how the splints and sterile tape worked together. She told Meg that the previous purchaser was about to bring the new system in but ran out of time before her departure.

Rick noticed that Meg looked somewhat distracted while Sally was talking. If Sally noticed, she ignored it, continuing on with her spiel.

Meg checked on her existing splint and tape inventory and told Sally the hospital wasn't actually low on tape at the moment. But Sally had made up her mind that she wasn't going to leave without an order. She urged Meg to buy some tape today because it was on sale for a short time, and that was what her predecessor always did.

Meg was simply overwhelmed in the face of Sally's assertive style. It was clear to Rick that Meg would do anything to get the meeting closed. She finally gave in to Sally and agreed to order some Bactogone tape.

Victorious, Sally strutted back to Rick's car. As they headed back to the office, she remarked, "I succeeded in earning her trust right from the beginning, don't you think?"

Rick was cautious. "I can see why you're selling so much in your first month. You're obviously pleased about getting Meg to buy just then."

Sally was feeling pretty good about it. "I try to stay focused on my goals."

But Rick had a question. "Now that we're leaving the hospital, how much of that tape do you think the staff will actually use?"

Sally shrugged her shoulders. "How would I know? I'm not in contact with anyone on the nursing staff."

Rick invited her to look at the bigger picture. He said, "It's nice that Meg stocked the hospital up with plenty of sterile tape.

But you won't be earning your big commissions, of course, until nurses actually pull our tape off the shelf and use it up."

"Yes, that's definitely true," Sally replied. "But I can't be there when nurses are deciding which tape to use."

Rick exclaimed, "You got it! A sale's real test is determined by what takes place after the salesperson leaves."

LAW #5:

THE REAL TEST OF A SALESPERSON'S INFLUENCE IS DETERMINED BY THE CUSTOMER'S ACTIONS AFTER THE SALESPERSON LEAVES.

Sally reluctantly agreed. "Well, sure. But my buyer has no real influence over the product's use. I doubt Meg ever speaks to the end users, the nurses."

Rick smiled. "Precisely! That's why this principle is so important and requires a salesperson's attention to its implications. Much of a salesperson's success depends on a customer's decision making in the salesperson's absence. Just about every company with a product or service relies on its customers to independently perform after the sale is over. This performance could be in the form of reusing, reordering, referring that product or service to others, or remaining loyal when approached by competitors. The customer's decision to reuse a product takes place internally, without a salesperson around reminding them. In Meg's case, it involves her following up on the use of our splints and tape after her purchase."

Sally replied, "Okay, I understand. I shouldn't congratulate myself just yet. Selling the tape to Meg doesn't necessarily mean the nurses will use it."

Rick took the opportunity to deepen Sally's understanding. "The most successful salespeople don't succeed in just getting the sale. They also succeed in having their customers internalize the sale. A sale that's internalized will influence the customer's decisions concerning the product long after the sale is over. The less a decision is based on the salesperson, the more internalized it will be."

He pointed out, "When you think about it, there are actually two conversations happening simultaneously within every sale. There's an external selling conversation between the salesperson and the customer. There's also an internal buying conversation taking place between the customer's ears. The salesperson's commission is determined by the internal buying conversation. The internal buying conversation determines whether the salesperson gets the sale at all. It will also determine how the customer will use that product or service after the sale is over and the salesperson is gone.

LAW #6:

THE LESS A SALESPERSON'S PERSUASION WAS INVOLVED IN A BUYING DECISION, THE MORE INTERNALIZED THE CUSTOMER'S DECISION WILL BE.

Sally inquired, "What exactly do you mean by 'internalized'?"

"Internalized decisions are decisions customers feel are truly their own," Rick replied. "There are important differences between internalized buying decisions and buying decisions made just because of a salesperson's recommendation. It's like the difference between a child taking his jacket to school because his Mom told him to and a child taking his jacket to school because he doesn't want to be cold. With internalized decisions, customers will take full responsibility and ownership for the decision's success. Salespeople should want their customers' buying decisions to be made as internally as possible."

Sally flashed to the power struggle she'd had that morning with her seven-year-old daughter about brushing her teeth twice a day. She was becoming intrigued with Rick's unusual sales thinking.

Rick gave her a moment to absorb this before querying, "I'm wondering something. How pleased with buying the product do you think Meg is? On a scale of one to ten, with ten being the best, how good do you think Meg felt about her decision to buy the tape?"

Sally was surprised by the question. "Why would that be important? I got the sale!"

Rick replied, "I'm not saying you should have done anything differently. Let's see how much we can learn from what we observed about Meg."

Sally thought back to the interaction. She hadn't seen any signs of enthusiasm from Meg throughout the exchange and had felt that it was difficult to engage Meg in conversation.

Rick asked, "Did Meg ask the kinds of questions that you would have asked if you were in her position?"

"No, she seemed a little distracted," Sally replied.

Rick agreed. "I thought so, too."

Sally said, "Okay, I'll give her a three out of ten for feeling good about buying the tape." She added, "That's totally a guess. She may just not be an expressive person."

Rick said, "I'd also guess three." He paused for a moment. "All things being equal, I think you'd agree it's preferable for Meg to feel good about her decision to buy our tape today."

Sally wasn't so sure. "I really don't see why it matters very much. I got the sale, and that's what counts."

Rick gently continued, "What you're saying is true. What's also true is that Meg is new on the job and still learning the ropes. As a purchaser, her job is to make buying decisions all day long. How she feels about her new purchasing position depends, to some degree, on how well she feels she's doing her job. If she feels good about her purchases, she'll feel good about her job. If you helped her feel good about her competence as a purchaser, I'm sure she'd be eager to meet with you in the future. And you'd probably feel good about that as well?"

"Sure, I'd like Meg to look forward to my visits. I want her to like me. Do you think she liked me?"

Rick took a beat. "I'm not sure it matters quite the way you think it might. Like most salespeople, you've probably been taught that getting customers to like you is the major component for getting the sale. If the customer doesn't buy, salespeople presume they haven't sufficiently established rapport. But I question that presumption. I think customers buy primarily because they feel the product or service will be best for them. Their opinion about the salesperson plays a minor role. In fact, there's a general tendency for people to feel overly responsible for the actions of others. I think it's only human nature to do so. We all tend to overestimate the role we play in what people around us say and do."

Sally was listening closely.

Rick continued, "This overestimation of our own impact results in a misperception about how we are affecting, or failing to affect, others. And, of course, that misperception has consequences. For example, think how easy it is to misperceive that people whispering nearby are probably talking about us. In reality, their conversation probably has nothing to do with us at all. The unintended consequence of that misperception is that we might become suspicious of them and may even decide to avoid those people altogether. Our decision to avoid them, however, will be erroneous because it's based on a false premise. I believe this human tendency is why salespeople overestimate their influence on customers' decisions."

"Yes, I'm familiar with the behavior you're talking about," Sally replied. "It's probably a major contributor to prejudice in the world. But I'm not seeing how this relates to selling."

Rick elaborated. "I can remember lots of times I've purchased products from salespeople I didn't particularly like. There are also plenty of times I purchased a product from one salesperson even though I liked a different salesperson better. I bought from the one I liked less because I thought he or she had a better product for me."

Sally's wheels were beginning to turn. "Yeah, that makes sense, when you think about it. A part of me always suspected that phrase about salespeople needing to sell themselves was overblown."

Rick exclaimed, "Yes! It's missing the point! Following that wrong concept leads salespeople to overestimate the extent to which their customers' decisions revolve around them. An unintended consequence is the distraction it creates for customers when they're in the middle of trying to make an important buying decision. A self-centered salesperson who's busy trying to steal the limelight just ends up distracting his customer from focusing on the product and making a good decision."

Sally interjected, "Okay, that makes sense, but how does all this apply to my sales call with Meg? Are you saying I was too self-centered with Meg?"

Rick replied, "No. You were very patient and empathetic with Meg, considering she's just getting acclimated to her new purchasing job. We both noticed, however, that Meg looked somewhat distracted while you were talking to her. She may have based her order more on your recommendation than on her own understanding of our tape's unique benefit."

Rick continued, "When you think about it, salespeople probably wouldn't even want to be the primary basis for a customer's buying—even if they could be. In general, I'd prefer that my customers buy for their own reasons rather than for reasons that came from me."

Sally could see it, too. "It makes sense."

Rick had another observation. "The relationship my customers develop toward the product is much more important than the relationship they develop toward me. Their relationship with the product will determine the long-term success of my sales, long after I'm gone. When I jump in with a bunch of reasons for my customer to buy, chances are I'm steering them away from reasons they were about to come up with on their own."

Sally: "Whoops!"

Rick continued, "Customer-derived reasons to buy are always going to be better than ones that I offer. This is consistent with my Sixth Law of Selling To The Point: The less a salesperson's persuasion was involved in a buying decision, the more internalized the customer's decision will be."

Sally exclaimed, "Rick, do you realize that what you're saying flies in the face of everything most salespeople believe? Salespeople are completely immersed in the belief that they need to control the sales process."

Rick replied, "I know it's an unusual thing to say, and I'm not really asking you to change or do anything differently. I'm just here to point things out about the customer. You get to decide what the best way to respond will be. But I think you'll find, if you play with this a little, that the more you try to take over the interaction, the less will get revealed to you about your customer. As your trainer watching you talk so much that the customer doesn't get a word in edgewise, I won't have many observations about the customer to share with you."

Rick suddenly changed direction. "Where did you work before coming to Essentials?"

Sally replied, "I was a travel agent. I sold vacation packages, cruises, even some medical tourism trips. Medical tourism is when people go to another country to get their surgery done. It's a lot less expensive if you're willing to assume some risk."

"That's interesting," Rick replied. "How long did you do that?"

"Four years."

"How did you know which packages to recommend when you first started?"

"I hadn't previously done much travel," Sally told him. "I needed to ask around with a lot of questions at first."

"I suppose you had to do a lot of listening to the answers you got as well."

"That's true. I'd ask other agents at the office, I'd get information from the touring companies, and I'd get feedback from clients who went on the trips."

"Which helped the most?"

"The customer's experience was the most valuable, of course," Sally said. "They gave me the best perspective of how the tours really were."

Rick agreed. "Me too. Whenever I started with a new company, talking to existing customers provided me with the most insight about how to sell the product. These customers had experienced using the product firsthand and truly believed in it.

There's no substitute for exposing new salespeople to that level of conviction."

Sally agreed. "Really."

"When salespeople volunteer selling points, customers have an easier time dismissing the selling points as uncompelling. The same selling points wouldn't be dismissed as easily if the customer came up with them on his or her own. For example, I put myself through college as a local club tennis instructor. My mom was a member of that club. I attempted to drag her on the court to give her lessons, but she wouldn't improve because she didn't follow my instructions after the lesson was over. Then a funny thing happened. Other members of the club started beating her. They told her it was because they had taken my lessons.

"Suddenly, Mom took the initiative to ask me for tennis lessons! She instantly became the fastest-learning student I ever had. So look at how my mom made her buying decision—when she independently decided I should teach her tennis. The same instruction that previously hadn't worked suddenly became transformational. My instruction was the same; the difference was in her receptivity. My instruction wasn't effective until she independently came up with the idea to have me teach her.

"There it is—it's always preferable to have customers, rather than salespeople, come up with reasons to buy. This is the case even with the same selling point a salesperson was going to make."

"I'm beginning to get it."

"Salespeople may think they sound smart when they offer a bunch of selling points, but they're missing the point," Rick added. "The point of selling is the customer's decision to buy. Customers can't dismiss reasons to buy that they came up with on their own. A salesperson who withholds selling points until customers discover them on their own may not sound as smart. However, she'll get a lot more sales."

Sally said, "I'm getting the point. It's about buying, not selling. I like it."

"I try to grant customers the autonomy to focus attention on whatever they feel leads to the best decision," Rick told her. "This way, they'll feel that I'm on their side."

Sally said, "That reminds me of those salespeople who try to put on a show. It makes me think there must be something wrong with the product if the salesperson wants me looking at them instead of at the product."

"Exactly," Rick responded. "Salespeople think they're gaining favor with customers by putting on a whole show, but they're actually creating suspicion. Customers get suspicious about why salespeople need to distract their attention from the product. Good relationships develop in an environment where it's okay for each party to think whatever they want to think about the other party. Salespeople who trust customers with whatever impression the customer chooses to have of them are the salespeople who enjoy the best rapport."

"Some of this could be tough for me," Sally admitted. "It's not that this doesn't make sense. It does. It's just that I have a difficult time picturing myself letting sales calls unfold differently than I had planned."

"Yeah," Rick agreed. "Control of sales calls is a universal ambition. Salespeople want customers to like them because they think it gives them more control.

"They're missing the point. Salespeople may gain more control over a customer's opinion of them, but that's unlikely to be what the buying decision will be based on. The customer's buying decision will probably be based on the customer's opinion of the product rather than of the salesperson."

Sally sighed. "That's a lot to let go of. I put a lot of work into being liked. So how do you suggest I handle the situation with Meg?"

"We talked about the importance of your customer's decision making," Rick told her. "This means we want to turn our focus around and look at Meg's buying situation rather than at our selling situation. Neither of us knows exactly what got Meg to buy the tape. However, we did notice she didn't seem very present or engaged with her decision making. You may want to consider finding out more about her outlook on the new position she's in. You could ask her about perceived differences between her and the purchaser she replaced. The comparison could reveal where her attention tends to go. Notice which differences she tends to dwell on, because that will reveal what she thinks are priorities. It will provide guidance to you about aspects of her purchasing position that would potentially excite her. You're in a better position to benefit from paying close attention to Meg than most salespeople I train. You're a great observer. Your ability to assess that Meg's enthusiasm was only a three out of ten was very astute. Possessing the gift of accurate observation will allow you to accurately respond for the best result."

Sally said, "Thanks. Now that you mention it, I do get lots of sales from things I notice about customers."

They arrived back at the office. Sally thanked Rick for the insights and told him she was looking forward to her next training session. They agreed Hope General Hospital would be their best rendezvous spot. Sally left for home thinking about their conversation.

Sally was a little miffed when Ben asked her to meet with the company CFO, Martin. She was planning to go home early and make prospecting phone calls before her daughter came home from school. She made her way to Martin's office. When she walked back to accounting, she immediately noticed the contrast between the noisy and chaotic sales department and this quiet refuge where money was quietly accounted for. This was a place where she could actually make sales calls instead of having to go home.

Martin's office was all the way at the back of the suite. Stacks of papers sat on top of file cabinets. Martin's large desk had piles of papers all over it. She wondered how he could find anything.

Martin motioned for Sally to have a seat. She quickly sat down at the only chair without something on it. Martin said, "Thank you so much for meeting with me on such short notice. I'll be concise so you can get back to your customers. I'd like to know your impression of working with Rick yesterday. You came to the company with a lot of prior selling experience. I know his methods are unconventional, so I'd like to hear how helpful you feel the experience was."

Sally thought to herself, "So that's what this meeting is about? Wow, what a switch. Usually it's the company asking the trainer how the salesperson is doing."

She looked at him. "I appreciate that you value my opinion. I was impressed with Rick's training because he gave me things to think about that I hadn't considered before. At first, I felt the sales call we went on was pretty straightforward and routine. But afterward, Rick was able to provide insightful feedback. Most sales trainers in the same scenario would just have said, 'Good job,' and left things at that. And now we've agreed to have a follow-up appointment with the same client. I'm looking forward to it."

Martin felt disappointed that Sally's initial response didn't provide him with ammo he could use against Rick. He decided to try one more angle. He asked her, "What did he train you to say differently?"

"He didn't tell me to say or do anything differently," Sally replied. "We just talked about the importance of being a good observer and some other things to consider when selling. He plans on specifically showing me how to do those things during our follow-up appointment. He wanted to ensure my long-term success by getting reorders. Without reorders, I won't be able to make my vendor's numbers."

An exasperated Martin honored his promise to keep the meeting short. He thanked Sally for taking the time to speak with him. Sally said, "You're welcome" and left for home.

On the way home, Sally wondered if Rick knew the company's CFO was checking up on him. She decided it would be best to not discuss the conversation with Rick. She didn't want to get caught up in politics her first month on the job.

Martin wished his conversation with Sally had given him more to go on. Sally was positive about her training experience with Rick. She obviously felt Rick's training would help her sales in the long run. Martin thought it was significant, however, that she couldn't put her finger on what exactly Rick trained her to do differently. Maybe Rick intended to be more directive during the follow-up appointment with Sally. Martin also considered the possibility that Rick drew out his engagement by not giving salespeople concrete instructions.

Martin felt even more determined to prove the company could no longer afford to support a costly sales trainer.

Chapter 4

THEY CAN'T HEAR YOU OVER THE SALES PITCH
How Customers Decide to Buy

THE RAIN WAS COMING DOWN HARDER NOW, MAKING THE little Wayside Tavern on the outskirts of town look even more isolated than it really was. Rick dodged a few puddles in the parking lot, stepped inside, and peered into the gloom.

He saw the handsome lady he was looking for already seated at a corner table.

"Hey, Lila, it's been a while."

"Rick, you always look the picture of health. Maybe your supplements over at Essentials are better than ours…"

"Could be," Rick kidded back. "You know, no one forced you out."

Lila had been CFO at Essentials before she left for HealthNext—a parallel company except that HealthNext had offered her some equity, something Essentials never would.

They ordered drinks and caught up on industry news for a few moments, and then Lila came to the point.

"Rick, you know that I still stay in touch with Joan. I admired her when she was my CEO at Essentials, and I value her honest competition and friendship today."

"I'm a big fan, too," Rick murmured, wondering where this was headed.

"Joan told me there are some big changes coming to Essentials. Looking for outside investors, and needing to get aggressive with the balance sheet."

"I've seen some pressures here and there..." Rick confirmed.

Lila moved forward a tiny bit, creating an air of conspiracy. "Joan says she's under pressure to cut the sales training budget."

Rick was momentarily startled at her directness. "Well, maybe, but you know I can't really discuss—"

Lila cut him off. "Joan said it was okay to talk with you."

Rick knew Lila wouldn't lie to him—it was too short a circuit for him to get back to Joan. "Okay..."

Lila continued, "We're facing some of the same pressures as Essentials, what with energy prices unexpectedly going through the roof. Although we've played with the idea for years, maybe the time has come to look at bringing in more independent reps who would work part-time from home." She peered at Rick, looking for his reaction.

Rick ran the scenario and seemed to see some potential in it. "You'd end up with generally less professional salespeople, so there could be a lot of challenges."

"Like?"

"Like—part-timers are going to be lower key, slower, not closers, and maybe even a little resistant to traditional sales training."

"So what to do?"

"They would need a different kind of training, something along the lines of what I've been increasingly doing at Essentials. In this case, it would be even more necessary."

"Give me the elevator pitch."

Rick explained the basics of his concept that the point of selling is buying. "Salespeople who work at home are typically not hard closers. Many are stay-at-home moms or semiretired people looking to make a few extra bucks. Many don't even consider themselves salespeople. The idea of aggressively taking control of a sales call and attempting a hard close is something they'd find distasteful."

He laid out the case for how low-key, part-time salespeople would be more comfortable learning how to help their customers buy rather than learning how to pound on them.

Lila had heard enough of what she had hoped to hear. "Here's the deal, Rick. If Joan's forced to tighten her training budget and you're not going to be happy at Essentials, you've got a place at HealthNext. I can't pay you what you earn there right off the bat, and I know you still have two kids to put through college, but there's a big potential upside if sales increase over time."

Rick took a moment to consider what a pay cut would mean. When he considered all of his financial pressures, the idea of starting over at a new place didn't feel very appealing.

Rick said, "I really appreciate that, Lila. I would hate to leave Essentials, especially because it's where I was given the opportunity to develop my thinking. My sales team is really getting into it, and that's been enormously gratifying. But it's certainly nice to know I have a place to land should Essentials decide to let me go."

Lila shook his hand, creating an agreement of some kind. "I'll tell Joan we spoke."

She started to leave and turned around to say, "You know, Rick, if you left this town, you'd have a lot more options."

The next morning at Essentials, Martin double-checked his inbox, making sure he hadn't overlooked a message from Joan. On one hand, he was happy not to hear from her because he didn't have any news about how to handle Rick. But on the other hand, with the big changes happening in the organization, not hearing from his CEO made him antsy.

Suddenly, Ben knocked on his door and, without waiting for a formal invitation, popped his head in. "Got a moment?"

Martin grunted an assent, and Ben closed the door behind himself.

"Seems like your old buddy Lila was having a late evening conference with Rick last night."

Martin was momentarily taken aback. Anything involving his CFO predecessor was likely to tick him off because Lila had maintained her friendship with Joan. He blamed Lila for somehow getting in the way of his forming a strong bond with his boss.

"Is this for real? How do you know?"

Ben's brother was a bartender at the Wayside, but Ben was going to keep his cards close to his chest. "I have my sources. It's for real. Not only that, but they shook hands over something."

"Whoa. Why in the world might Lila be recruiting our sales trainer right at the time we're being forced to cut back? You know, when it comes to Lila, I just don't trust her. I mean, get real. She's dealing with the cost crisis just like we are. "

Ben gave him a look. "Maybe not just like we are. Maybe totally differently."

Martin felt like he was perpetually playing catch-up to Ben today. "Want to help me out?"

Ben drew a little closer. "I think I found what Lila's up to. And she would need Rick."

"Really?"

Ben continued, "After I heard about the meeting, I did a little research. HealthNext is running ads for work-at-home salespeople. I think Lila's answer to the cost crisis is to set up a home-based sales force."

Martin thought about that. "Boy, that's a big move. Home-based selling is an entirely different animal from professional field rep work. Huge learning curve, different type of salesperson, different environment. So why Rick?"

Ben replied, "Rick's approach is perfect for them. He trains salespeople so their customer's buying process can take the lead. Once salespeople are involved with the buying process, they can just respond to what's needed. This results in salespeople not being perceived as salespeople at all. They're functioning more like decision coaches."

"I wonder if Lila told Joan what she was up to," Martin wondered aloud.

"Hard to say. They can both be unpredictable."

Martin finally got a moment with Joan for a face-to-face.

Joan was focused on the big picture: financial reports and board meetings. "Look, Martin, I have meetings coming up with the board next week, and after that I'm on vacation for a week, so I'll need you to take the helm on preparing reports while I'm gone."

Martin was fine with that, but he still wanted to circle back to Rick.

"I hear Lila's been chatting with Rick. Is this a done deal?"

Joan was a little taken aback that word had spread so fast. "Well, I think it's great all around. We organize a seamless move out for Rick—no harm, no foul. Balance sheet looks better, and we're leaning down for the tough times ahead. I think Lila's doing us a big favor, actually."

Martin was ambivalent, but there was some upside for him, no question. "I'm glad I don't need to get blood on my hands."

Joan understood how much he hated firing anyone. "I was delighted to take that off your plate."

Martin left, but he wasn't all that happy. He deeply resented Lila and Joan taking away his control over financial decision making when it came to deciding Rick's fate.

And worst case, Lila might be right and he and Joan wrong. What if recruiting Rick suddenly put HealthNext on a fast track at the same time Essentials was cutting back?

Martin grabbed the phone when he got back to his office. "Ben? I need some hard numbers from you, and I need them now. I want to look at sales per salesperson for the ones Rick trained. And I want to see six months before and after."

Ben said, "I can do that."

Martin wasn't finished. "I need more. I need you to track down number of visits before and after Rick's training as well, per salesperson. I need to know if he really does cut down on the number of sales calls."

Ben was troubled by this one. "I dunno. We've never encouraged salespeople to make fewer visits. Maybe I can get some anecdotal for you."

"Well, that's better than nothing. And one thing more; I need to talk with Rick. Can you set up a lunch? It's urgent. Like tomorrow. If I'm going to sell Joan and the board on Rick's approach, then I need to get a better understanding of what Rick actually does."

The next day, Rick and Martin were lunching at the little sandwich shop across from the office that served as Essentials' virtual cafeteria.

Martin said, "It's funny that we've worked together for ten years but hadn't spoken until last week. Was the previous CFO more sociable than I am?"

Rick took the bait. "Lila and I had a pretty good connection. We're both from farm families. When I told her I learned from my father that sales could be cultivated like crops, it made a lot of sense to her."

"Sales and farming?" Martin asked. "You bonded over that?"

"Well, actually, yes. Mother Nature has endowed every plant with an elegant, complex, and natural growth process. I make it the salesperson's first priority to notice and appreciate the natural capacity for buying that customers are endowed with. Same thing."

"So nurture the customer the same as you would a plant," Martin replied. He resisted the desire to roll his eyes.

"That's the short form," Rick confirmed. "The actual doing takes training, but the yields are great." He went on, "The salesperson needs to give buyers what they need to make a comfortable—you could even say 'natural'—buying decision. Decisions based on motivating feelings can be just as compelling as cerebral-based decisions—perhaps even more so. The salesperson needs to be comfortable helping buyers shift from a strictly cerebral-based decision style in order to integrate their customer's feelings into the decision as well. Many salespeople are uncomfortable relating to customers in the realm of their feelings. This is understandable. It's easier to know what a customer's thinking than to know what they're feeling.

"Every decision to buy is ultimately connected to an underlying feeling. It could be the feeling of satisfaction a customer derives from being successful in business. It could also be the feeling of relief from an unpleasant feeling. But overly cerebral-based decision making can lead to analysis-paralysis. A customer could agree with a salesperson's thinking without buying."

Martin was thinking about his own problems. "So I'm trying to sell someone something at this very moment, and I'm wondering how I might succeed. I need to sell Joan on not letting you go off to HealthNext, and all she wants from me are numbers on sales budget and sales performance. There's no room in there for emotion."

Rick was surprised at the sudden turn in his own direction but was immediately intrigued by the challenge. "So Joan is focused on the demands of the board and on the need for good performance numbers right now, in the short term. Lila has the freedom to completely change her sales strategy to respond to a changing world. One is able to make a decision based on her feelings; the other is frozen in cerebral mode and will need endless numbers to help with her decision-making process. One is likely to make wise decisions; the other will likely be frozen because of fear."

Martin responded, "That pretty much describes it."

Rick was clear about the issues. "What's really going on is lack of trust. Joan doesn't trust herself, doesn't trust you enough, and doesn't even trust her numbers. Lack of trust can shift decision making from being feelings-oriented to being cerebral. Whenever customers lack trust, their decision-making style makes that shift."

Martin was still focused on Joan. "So how do I get Joan to shift her decision-making style?"

"Think about an inexperienced farmer just watering a plant's leaves because they look dry."

Martin laughed. "So Joan's a plant?"

Rick was undeterred. "She's *like* a plant. You shower her with reports. They don't get internalized. She needs knowledge and understanding at the roots—so she can make an integrated decision."

Martin knew Rick was telling him the truth. "So what do you suggest?"

Rick had a thought. "I've got to cover a sales call for one of our reps who is out sick. You can come along, and if it provides a strong story, you can tell it to Joan and start the feeding process."

Martin thought this was a little far-fetched, but he was beginning to feel that Rick had some weird, Zen-like sense of how things really worked.

An hour later, Martin and Rick arrived at the office of Serenity, a holistic medical practice. The practice consisted of seven doctors plus counselors and other alternative health-care professionals.

Rick and Martin introduced themselves to the receptionist, who pointed them to the purchaser's office.

Bernard invited them in, and Rick introduced Martin as someone making a career change who was in training.

Bernard was a sensitive soul and wanted to reassure Martin. "It's never too late to become a lifelong learner."

Martin wanted to growl at him, but instead gave him a nice smile and stayed in his role as sales trainee.

Rick began by asking Bernard a few general questions about the practice. During the conversation, Rick picked six bottles out of the case he'd brought and placed them on Bernard's desk. Bernard reached for one of the bottles as they were talking. Rick stopped talking as soon as Bernard examined the first bottle. Bernard picked up each bottle one by one and examined the long ingredient lists.

Martin felt uncomfortable with the long silence and wanted to interject his own comments, but he forced himself to hold back because he suspected Rick was up to something. Rick continued silently and patiently letting Bernard take as much time as he wanted to analyze each bottle's formula.

After Bernard put down the last bottle, he said, "Hmmm. Those products are interesting."

Rick replied, "Which one did you think was the most interesting?"

"This one. It's got Propolis. Very few people know about the antibiotic properties of bee Propolis, but we're big fans of it here."

"Was there anything else you saw about a product that sticks in your mind?"

"Not really," Bernard replied. "They all look interesting."

"Okay."

Rick selected two of the six bottles on Bernard's table and gave them a quick glance. Then he pulled a three-leaf binder full of supplement product labels out of his briefcase, flipped to the index, and turned to a page of labels.

"Have a look at these two labels from the new line of supplements that we have a lot of respect for," Rick said to Bernard.

Bernard took the label book and examined the two labels. As he put the book down, he said, "Yes, that's what I had in mind."

"Terrific," Rick said. "Each product comes in two sizes— 60 capsules and 120 capsules—which is either a two-week or one-month supply. Your price is $14.99 for the 60s and $21.99 for the 120s; the patient price is $29.99 and $43.99. Would you like to get your usual quantity of twelve, or would you like to start with twenty-four for 10 percent off?"

Bernard replied, "Can I get 10 percent off for twelve of the 60 capsules and twelve of the 120 capsules?"

"I can do that if you're planning on bringing in both products."

"Great, let's do it."

Once they got back in Rick's car, Martin said, "I didn't know you knew so much about holistic medicine."

"Actually, I don't know anything about holistic medicine," Rick told him. "Everything you saw happen was simply the power of good observation." He went on. "I didn't actually say anything about the products. Yesterday our rep, Claudio, who was getting ill, selected the six bottles I could put in front of Bernard. Each bottle had natural antibiotic ingredients that worked differently. Each of the six bottles represented a different natural antibiotic approach. I just watched carefully to see which bottles drew his attention the most. I also looked for any facial expressions that could indicate the type of impression a product left."

Martin interjected, "I was trying to read you reading him, but I couldn't get it."

Rick continued, "I especially took note of which bottles he analyzed the longest. He seemed most interested in two bottles in particular. He also signaled favorable response after he analyzed them. He mentioned the ingredient Propolis. I don't have any idea what that is, but I knew I should look for it in the products I picked. Once I took note of everything, I got out the label book and showed him two products matching the same method of action. I also made sure they contained Propolis."

Martin said, "Okay, I'm impressed! That was brilliant. Was that farming?"

"Absolutely," Rick replied. "I didn't interfere with or intervene in Bernard's natural decision-making process. I just supported it with the information he needed to make a good decision, just like a farmer supports a plant's natural growing process with what it needs and then gets out of the way. Natural processes will do best left on their own. Our job is to support them, not to intervene. Instead of being a farmer, I was being Bernard's decision coach."

Rick was thinking about a story Martin could take back to Joan. "My training doesn't focus on product knowledge the way most sales training does. For Essentials, I've greatly shortened the training time it takes to get our salespeople on the road."

Martin said, "I can't wait to tell Joan about what I saw today." Then Martin had another thought. "What do you know about softball?"

Rick grinned and answered, "About as much as I know about holistic medicine."

Martin smiled to himself. "Right. I've got a team I'm coaching. Maybe I'll bring you along one of these days."

"I'd love to try to help."

Chapter 5

THE UH-OH EFFECT
Enhancing a Decision's Desirability

MARTIN SPENT TUESDAY CONDUCTING DEPARTMENT MEETINGS. Most of the meetings' agendas involved informing supervisors about the decision that Essentials would seek outside investors. His Tuesday went by quickly as he explained what role each supervisor would be playing.

Martin was surprised to see that it was already 5:00 p.m. He was late for his daughter's softball game, which he was coaching. Her team, the Robins, was struggling to make the play-offs this year after a romp in the previous year. At the heart of the struggle was the Robins' once-star pitcher, Katya, who seemed to have lost her magic.

Martin had been training hard with Katya, but nothing was working. The harder she tried, the more her control fell apart. This year she was a disaster in pressure situations, which tended to feed on themselves. Even when Martin tried to keep the pressure off her and work with her to help her learn to relax, nothing helped.

Tonight, Rick had agreed to speak with Katya before the game. Martin was curious to see what, if any, magic Rick could work with a high school pitcher who had suddenly gone wild. Martin drove home and picked up his daughter, Fiona, and they headed over to the field.

At Fiona's age, being seen as too close to her father wasn't cool, so as soon as they got to the ball field, Fiona went her own way, ditching her dad and catching up with friends. Martin opened his trunk and dragged out the heavy burden of bats, balls, catcher gear, bases, and batting helmets. He dragged it all over to the stands, barely avoiding tripping in the middle of the dust storm he was creating.

And that's when he noticed Katya and her mom, Marnie, observing him with amused fascination.

"Looks like instant softball," Marnie observed. "Just add Coach Martin, a bit of dust, and stir."

Martin could laugh at himself. "I think we could use some assistant coaches around here!"

Katya and her mom were quite close, so Martin—now in his third year of coaching the Robins—was used to navigating Marnie while dealing with Katya's frustration. He addressed Katya. "If it's okay with you, I've got a super pitching coach coming by who may be able to give you a couple of pointers."

Katya wasn't so sure about that, but she assented. "Okay."

Then to Marnie, he said, "I really think this guy's got great insights."

What he really wanted to say was, "Are you free one of these evenings?" But he hadn't worked up the courage just yet. He knew Marnie was single and worked as a reporter on the local paper. And there was something about her.

Marnie was instinctively protective of Katya. "As long as he's not high-pressure."

Martin laughed. "Whatever the opposite of pressure is, that's what he is."

Rick had pulled into the parking lot and was now walking toward them.

"Hey, Rick, thanks for coming by," Martin said, and he made the introductions to Katya and her mom. "So I was mentioning to you our great starting pitcher here, Katya. She had a great season last year, but she's had some control issues this season."

"I'll do what I can to help," Rick replied warmly. He turned to Katya. "So Katya, what do you think is the problem?"

Katya gave a noticeable sigh and said, "I seem to have lost my control. Maybe it's something I'm doing wrong this year."

Rick looked at her and said, "Who knows? I'll tell you what, Katya. I promise not to be one of those annoying coaches who tell you what to do. I'm going to let you decide if you want to change anything or not. Is that a deal?"

Katya relaxed a bit and made eye contact with Rick. "Sure."

61

Rick shooed Martin and Marnie off of the mound, and when he and Katya were alone, he motioned to the catcher to get behind the plate. Then Rick turned to Katya and casually said, "Okay, Katya, why don't you show me a pitch or two."

Katya said, "Okay."

She made three pitches. Each one was fast and straight, hitting the catcher's glove with a satisfying slap.

Rick strolled over to the mound. "What do you notice about your pitching?"

"I'm letting the team down," Katya told him. "I'm just not pitching as well this year as I was last year. I don't know what's wrong."

"Hmmm, that doesn't sound very fun," Rick responded. "Tell me more about this pitching difference."

"Last season, everything seemed to be going right. There were some games I pitched so well that I felt the ball was finding the strike zone by itself. This year, I'm missing the same pitches I could trust to strike batters out last year. Martin tells me I'm not taking my wrist back far enough before releasing the pitch. He said that's why my old pitches had more snap in them than they have this year. I tried listening to him by taking my wrist back more. It isn't helping, though."

Rick asked, "Would you mind if I ask a batter to stand in?"

"Sure."

Martin rounded up a batter to stand at home plate and then quietly inched close to the pitcher's mound so he could stay within earshot of Rick coaching Katya.

Rick said, "All right, Katya, show me a pitch that's not going well this year but was fine last year."

"Okay, I'll try a high and inside pitch."

Rick said, "That means you're aiming for the right side of the plate and just below the batter's shoulders, right?"

"Right," Katya responded. She threw three pitches and then looked over at Rick.

Rick asked her, "What do you think about those pitches?"

"Only one of them was in the strike zone. The other two pitches missed. Last year, I could count on never missing a high and inside pitch."

"Are you sure the problem is with your wrist and not your arm?" Rick asked her.

Katya replied, "No. I didn't think my arm was a problem."

"I'm not sure if it's actually a problem or not. Let's take a closer look. Are you aware of how far back your arm goes before it moves forward to throw?"

"No," Katya told him. "I hadn't thought about it before."

"Let's have a look," Rick suggested. "Throw a few more pitches. Don't change anything you normally do. Just notice how far back your arm goes before you bring it forward to pitch."

Katya threw three pitches. Each time, she took note of how far back her arm went before she moved it forward.

"What did you notice?" Rick asked her.

"My arm goes back to here." She pointed to the farthest position that she took the ball back to.

Rick said, "Okay, now throw a few more high and inside pitches. This time, let me know if you always take your arm to that spot or if it's a little different for each pitch."

"Okay."

She threw four high and inside pitches. Rick observed that at least three of them seemed to be in the strike zone. Katya hadn't noticed this. She was more focused on her pitching motion.

Katya said, "I seem to take them all back just as far."

"That's fine," Rick replied. "It looked that way to me, also. Now I want you to pitch a few more balls and notice when you release the ball."

Katya asked him, "Is there something wrong with my release?"

"Not necessarily. Every pitcher has a slightly different style. Let's take a closer look at yours." He tossed a ball to her.

Katya threw three more pitches. She noticed the feeling of releasing each pitch. Once again, she didn't pay much attention to where the pitches landed. She was busy noticing the feeling of her release instead.

Rick asked, "How did the release feel to you on those pitches?"

"The release on every pitch felt fine."

"I didn't see a problem with them either," Rick told her. "Now let's put them together. I want you to notice the moment your arm is completely back and say the word 'stop.' I also want you to notice the moment when you release the ball, and say the word 'go' when you release it. The goal of this exercise is to simultaneously say the words 'stop' and 'go' exactly at the moment the action happens. We won't worry about where the pitches land right now. We can look at that later."

Katya gave Rick a curious look as he handed her a ball. She pitched it and said, "Stop" when her arm went back and "go" as she released the ball.

Rick asked her, "Did you say stop and go simultaneously to the motion?"

"I'm not sure. Probably not."

"Here, throw another pitch and tell me about this one," Rick said.

She threw another pitch, trying more carefully to synch the words with the action.

Rick said, "I noticed you synched the words with the action more accurately that time. Here, try a few more pitches."

He tossed her one ball after another for eight pitches. Each time, Katya focused on synching the words stop and go with her pitches.

"How do you think you did?" Rick asked.

"I timed the words stop and go best for the last few pitches."

"I noticed that as well," he told her. "What percentage of inside and high pitches land in the strike zone for you so far this year?"

"I'm not sure," Katya replied. "I think I only get about one in the strike zone for every four pitches."

"Do you know how many inside and high pitches you pitched in the strike zone this exercise?"

"No, not exactly," Katya answered. "I was too busy paying attention to saying the words. That's what you told me to do."

Rick replied, "Yes, it is what I asked you to do. However, I was looking at where your pitches went. Every one of your last five pitches was in the strike zone. The more you synched your words with your actions, the better your pitches were."

"Wow," Katya exclaimed. "Does that mean my timing is the problem?"

"Your timing isn't necessarily the problem. It's more about the *awareness* of your timing. Martin mentioned you have more trouble during the most important games."

"Yes, that's right," Katya said.

"That's because thinking about the importance of the game distracts you from pitching well. Thinking about where you want your pitches to go distracts you from paying attention to the pitch itself. This interference gets worse for the more important games."

"So you're saying that I'm not supposed to think about where the pitch should go?"

"The most important thing is to pay attention to the pitch itself," Rick replied. "You were getting pitches into the batter's box just fine even though you weren't paying much attention to where the pitches landed. Focus on the pitch itself rather than on where you think it should go."

"Okay, I'll try that. Thanks, Rick! Will you be coaching me before the next game as well?"

"I'd like to," Rick told her, "but I don't think you need my coaching. Your pitching is fine just the way it is. I didn't tell you to change anything about your pitching, did I?"

"No, you actually didn't," Katya replied.

"You're doing fine on your own. I don't see anything you need to change."

"You're right!" Katya said. "I'm glad my pitching's fine after all. Now I'm stoked about tonight's game."

"I'll stick around awhile. I can't wait to see how it goes," Rick told her.

Katya walked off the mound to check in with her mom, and Martin joined Rick.

"That was great! You coached her to pitch without knowing anything about softball."

"I told her she didn't need me because she did fine on her own," Rick remarked. "She was doing all the work, and what she got out of that was the thing she needed most—confidence. If I took any credit for it, then I'd be getting in the way."

"That sounds like what you've been saying about internalized decision making. The advantage of internalized decisions is that they endure after the salesperson is gone. This allows the customer's relationship with the product to continue without requiring the salesperson's intervention."

Rick was pleased. "Yes. You got it!"

"What made you decide that getting her focus on taking her arm back would be the best solution?" Martin asked.

"You said that Katya's pitching gets worse during the most important games," Rick replied. "I call that the uh-oh effect. Performers fall prey to that when their focus shifts to what they're trying to avoid. They end up doing exactly what they're most afraid of."

"So your solution was to change her focus of attention?" Martin asked him.

"Yes, I needed to get her attention back on the task itself rather than on the consequences of failing at the task. I could have asked her to focus on her grip, on the body language of the hitter, or on where she stood on the mound. Any one of these things would have worked."

"How does that apply to selling?"

"Salespeople need to coach their customers to make decisions without allowing the uh-oh effect to interfere—in a buying decision, that is the fear of making a bad decision," Rick responded. He went on. "You know what peak experience is, right?"

Martin had learned about the sixties in college. "Sure, it means being in the groove, or the flow..."

"Exactly. Now peak experience can be described as shy. It won't appear when expectations are present. If you want it, it won't show up. So I was able to solve the problem for Katya by shifting her attention back to the task at hand. That task at hand was the physical act of pitching, which is really what her performance is based on. I did that by getting her interested in her pitching motion. The increased spontaneity allows peak experience to enter."

"And in selling?" Martin asked.

"Self-doubt interferes with decision-making performance, just as it interferes with any other performance. Customers who doubt their ability to make good buying decisions will not attain peak experience while making decisions. Peak experience during decision making requires confidence. Confidence makes decision making enjoyable and clear, and it leads to successful results."

"This really is fascinating," Martin replied. "Your ideas would help me tremendously with my investor reports. Is there any way you can put this together for me as a simple system that would help me explain your training to others?"

Rick wasn't sure he could boil it down that far, but he said he'd try. "And let me know how Katya does in the game."

"I can't wait to find out myself!"

Chapter 6

THE MONSTER UNDER THE BED
The Importance of Decision-Making Quality

AFTER THE GAME, MARTIN HAD A MOMENT TO CHAT WITH Katya's mom, Marnie. He managed to find the courage to ask her out for coffee after the game, but Marnie instantly turned cool and said she needed to work with Katya on her homework. Martin was left on the field alone, picking up the bases.

At work Wednesday morning, Martin was still contemplating the Robins' win at the previous night's softball game. Katya was suddenly performing like the great pitcher she had been last year. The success was great, but he still felt some hurt at Marnie's swift rejection. What had turned her off? He almost wished Rick could coach him on Marnie.

But that was not going to happen. What he did wonder was where else within Essentials he might appropriately put Rick's special skills to work. He picked up the phone.

"Rick? Martin here. First off, you're a softball genius. Katya was on her *A game*, the team was inspired, and we won at an away game. Maybe we'll have you over for one of our games again before the end of the season.

"Now, look, I've got a special favor to ask. I stuck my neck out and offered a sales job to my nephew Carlos. He's got some experience and some great skills, but things somehow aren't clicking for him here. Maybe you could turn him around."

Rick replied, "Sure, he was on my list. I'll push him to next up of new hires. I believe I have an opening tomorrow. What do you think his issue is?"

"Well," Martin replied, "I don't know if it's any one thing. Carlos just seems to be struggling. Before he came here, he was selling medical devices for a couple of years, and he wasn't all that great there, either. Now his sales here are in the tank, and I'm afraid the vendor he represents will start complaining."

"Hmmm."

Martin tried to offer more clarity. "I'm perplexed because he's very motivated, and he has one of those perfect personalities for sales."

"Interesting. And what is it about Carlos's personality that makes him perfect for sales?" Rick inquired.

"Well, he's outgoing, assertive, almost aggressive," Martin replied. "He's goal-oriented and never shies away from a good argument. I thought his personality would persuade people to think his way."

Rick took a moment. "Well, those qualities might be helpful somewhere…"

Martin went on, "As I heard myself say it, I could also hear your gears grinding. Based on what you've been showing me, his personality may not be as much of an asset as I once thought."

"Maybe it's a little like Katya's problem—focusing more on the outcome than on the process necessary to attain it."

"Please, give it a try," Martin requested. "And then let me know what you think." He thanked Rick again, and they hung up.

Carlos got the news from Martin about his upcoming training from Rick and reacted well. He prepared for the next day by studying up on his newest products, a line of clinical thermometers known for their ability to withstand any type of sterilization without losing accuracy or durability.

The next morning, Carlos knocked on Rick's door and introduced himself. Rick appraised Carlos, noting the firm handshake and glowing demeanor. Carlos was short with dark hair and a thin mustache. His suit was casual beige, topped off with a bolo tie. Rick couldn't remember the last time he'd seen someone in his late twenties wear a bolo tie.

"So where are you taking me today?" Rick asked him.

"I was thinking we could call on one of my medical supply distributors—Bohm Medical. Bohm's purchases have gone flat this past year, and I can't figure out why. My buyer's name is Larisa. I arranged an appointment for the two of us to meet with her."

Rick nodded. "Excellent."

"I told her you're coming along as my trainer. Larisa's been at Bohm for a couple of years, but we have quite a few thermometers that should be in their catalog and aren't. My goal is to load them up on our latest model of thermometer, the Q1016 that just came out yesterday. I want to be the first one to get a sale with it."

Rick cautiously noted, "Coming out yesterday is new indeed. Has your vendor developed all the sales materials yet?"

"I was able to get the first draft of its manual, and I'm up to speed on it," Carlos told him.

"Okay, let's see how it goes. I'm sure the vendor will appreciate your feedback about how the Q1016 thermometer was received by your first customers."

At Bohm, Carlos jumped out of the car and headed to the reception desk. It took everything Rick had to keep up. Carlos announced himself to the receptionist, who buzzed Larisa. When the receptionist gave them the all-clear signal, Carlos seemed to already be headed down the hall toward Larisa's office. He waited by her office door for Rick to catch up. Carlos gave a few loud knocks and entered almost before Larisa could say, "Come in." Larisa was sitting behind her desk. She had two chairs waiting on the other side of the desk, which she'd set up in anticipation of her meeting with Carlos and Rick.

Carlos began the meeting by saying to Larisa, "Thank you for meeting with us today."

Larisa replied with an uncommitted, "You're welcome."

Carlos continued. "Larisa, this is Rick. He's the company trainer who I mentioned would be joining us."

Larisa said, "I'm pleased to meet you, Rick." She extended her arm and shook Rick's hand.

Carlos was not big on small talk, apparently. "I'm very excited today to show you our new line of thermometers."

Larisa sat back without saying anything and let Carlos continue.

He loaded up his right arm with a stack of brochures. "Each thermometer comes with its own technical manual." He placed eight manuals on Larisa's desk and continued talking. "Our newest and best thermometer is this one, the model Q1016." He picked that thermometer's manual out of the eight on her desk and handed it to her.

Carlos then began a very detailed description of the ways this model Q1016 thermometer was superior to the other brands. His presentation included the latest advances in thermocouple technology versus the RTD probes used in other devices; the improvements included increased accuracy, better Callendar–Van Dusen coefficient values for resistance, and the linearization capabilities of its advanced microprocessor. Rick was impressed with Carlos's knowledge of the Q1016's technical aspects. Larisa was thumbing through the Q1016 manual while Carlos was talking. Rick noticed she hadn't stopped thumbing through the manual long enough to read any of its pages. Once Larisa had glanced through the manual, she put it down with a sigh and turned her attention back to Carlos.

Carlos finished his presentation and said, "As a result of this superior technology, these thermometers will last twice as long as the other brands you carry. They'll withstand any type of steril-ization without compromising accuracy. A minimum order—a case of fifty Q1016 thermometers—would normally be $1,749.50, which works out to $34.99 each. However, for six cases, I'll bring the price down to $29.99 each, which totals out to $8,997.00. At six cases, you'll be paying only 20 percent more for a thermometer that lasts 50 percent longer. Would you like to start with one case, or would you like to get the extra value with six cases?"

"I'm not in a position to commit to a quantity today," Larisa replied. "I'll check with some other people here and let you know. Today I'll just repeat my usual semiannual order of three boxes of the P829 thermometers. That should hold me over until I can educate our engineers about the Q1016's superiority. Can I keep the manual for reference?"

Rick could see Carlos's shoulders visibly drop in disappointment. Carlos couldn't believe his great offer to Larisa was getting turned down in front of Rick. Carlos began to repeat his offer by saying, "But the Q1016 gives you twice the lifespan for only $29.99. That's just a five-dollar difference."

"Yes, I know," Larisa replied. "It's just that I have to get the engineers behind it, and they're a skeptical group."

"Even if you buy only one case, the difference would be just $10.00 per thermometer."

Larisa visibly stiffened. "Well, today I can just reorder my usual three cases of the P829s."

Larisa's body language looked to Rick like she was ready for them to leave, and he decided to jump in. "Those engineers are not only skeptical, but I imagine they can sometimes be downright arrogant about their technical expertise."

Carlos was happy just to sit back and watch Rick in action. He hoped Rick had a plan to salvage the situation.

"Yes, you have *that* right," Larisa told him. "They seem to relish the opportunity to show me I'm not as smart as they are, every chance they get."

"I can see that there's a lot involved for you when deciding on bringing in a new thermometer," Rick went on. "The model Q1016 is new for us, too. As a matter of fact, it just came out yesterday. The manual Carlos showed you is just a first draft that isn't even finalized, so I'm sure the information in it isn't yet all that clear. I couldn't help but notice when you were thumbing through it that nothing seemed to grab you. Do you have any suggestions for us in terms of making it a more useful tool for buyers like you?"

"Funny you should ask," Larisa said. "Actually, I was looking for a simple list of the important new features. The whole manual, the way it is now, is way too complicated. I'd never have time to go through it."

"So it had more information than you think someone in your position would need to make a good decision?"

"Yes, that's right," Larisa responded. "Too much information, most of which seems pretty unimportant. Being given too much information makes it harder to decide if the model Q1016 is actually a better value."

Rick handed the manual back to her and asked, "What types of things in this manual do you think we could remove?"

Larisa took the manual from Rick. She looked more relaxed as she quickly thumbed through it and then pointed to a page in the manual. "I don't need to know about the history of the copper and platinum used for thermocouple alloys," she said. "I just need to know that thermocouple technology works within a larger range of temperatures and has a faster response time than RTD."

Rick reached over and struck out the offending paragraphs with a pencil. "Done and done. Is there anything else you suggest we get rid of?"

Larisa replied carefully, measuring her words now that she was in charge of the editing process. "Well, actually, I don't need to see all these linearization coefficients. I just need to know that the alloys being used have a good linear relationship for temperature and resistance."

"I see what you're saying," Rick told her. Again, he reached across and struck out a bunch of verbiage. "Thanks, that feedback will help us. You actually understand this stuff better than most of our salespeople would."

"Hmmm, I suppose I did pick up a few tidbits of knowledge after all."

"When you think about it," Rick added, "just those two advantages alone would be enough to justify replacing the old thermometers with the new model to management. They'll be impressed with your ability to make buying decisions about technical products. And the new Q1016 is just 20 percent more!"

"I can see that, too," Larisa responded. "You know what? I'll take a six-case order of the Q1016 thermometers. Those engineers are always wanting the newest, latest gadgets anyway."

"Great," Rick said.

Carlos wrote up the order.

Back on the road, Rick said to Carlos, "I'm very impressed with how well you understand the technical aspects of those thermometers."

"Yes, thanks. But I can see it didn't help me get the sale."

"Today's appointment reminds me of an experience I recently had babysitting my four-year-old granddaughter," Rick told him. "The other night, she was scared of monsters under her bed and didn't want the light off.

"Now, if I had told her there's nothing to be afraid of, I would be making things worse. She would feel I didn't understand. So instead, I agreed with her that monsters are scary. I asked her to describe what monsters are like. She said they were big and loud. I replied, 'Then we would hear a big monster. I'll just chase it away as soon as I hear it.' And with the monster now under close watch, she was able to have the light off and go to sleep.

"So with Larisa, I used what I learned from my granddaughter. I observed her thumbing through the manual while you were talking. She didn't read anything. She looked at it with a sigh, like all the information in there was an 'uh-oh.' An 'uh-oh' is a factor that suddenly makes a task seem much more difficult. Later on, we found out the uh-oh was about having to justify her purchasing decision to the engineers. She was dreading the prospect of getting pummeled with 'gotcha' questions. And all the additional technical information she heard from you ended up supporting that fear."

"But I need to show her that I know what I'm talking about," Carlos said. "That's how I'll get her to trust and respect me."

"I understand," Rick replied. "But I don't think much of her decision making was going to be based on her trust and respect for you. I think it was more about her self-trust."

"Self-trust?"

"Larisa obviously wasn't confident about repeating your technical presentation to justify her purchase to the engineers," Rick explained. "And she wasn't going to buy until she was. I had to take the uh-oh away. I started with the disclaimer that we understood the manual wasn't designed to be understandable yet. I made it okay for her to not understand the information."

"I was wondering why you said that," Carlos said after a short pause. "I was concerned you were making us sound incompetent. It was like you were admitting we didn't have our act together yet for creating a good manual."

"Customers will always interpret our statements more in terms of what it means about them than what it means about us," Rick replied. "I knew it would be an uphill battle for her to be confident about understanding the Q1016 unless I removed the uh-oh. For my granddaughter, I needed to agree that monsters are scary."

Carlos was tracking Rick's logic. "And for Larisa?"

"Larisa was able to relax when I showed that I understood how confusing the manual could be. Once her uh-oh, her monster, was out of the way, she was able to get a clear picture of what she understood so far. So when I asked her for suggestions about what to take out, she began to realize that there was already a lot she did understand. And she demonstrated that to herself as she helped me cut down the manual."

Carlos frowned as he pondered what his gut would have had him do. "So what would have happened if I'd just straight out asked her how much she got from what I said?"

"Good question. The problem is, asking a direct and maybe even challenging question can create another uh-oh, which would increase Larisa's fear that she hadn't really grasped what you'd told her—especially because she fears that she'd expose her own lack of a strong technical background.

"When I asked her a question about an area in which she felt safe—by asking her which part of our manual was too technical—she could jump right in. It's always better for salespeople to be learners than to be teachers."

LAW #7:

IT'S BETTER FOR SALESPEOPLE TO BE LEARNERS THAN TO BE TEACHERS.

"Then how will customers learn, if they're the teacher and we're the learner?" Carlos asked. "I know a lot more about the Q1016 thermometer than Larisa does."

"Larisa was unable to make a buying decision because, way down deep, she was holding an objection that she could barely understand, let alone tell you about. And the source of that objection was?"

Carlos wanted to be right, so he thought hard about the answer he thought Rick was looking for. "Fear of some kind?"

Rick smiled. "You got it. Larisa believed that her knowledge was inadequate and that if she made a decision, it could easily be the wrong one. So she was frozen by this fear. Any offer you could make, no matter how terrific, was always going to get a 'no' because it was impossible for her to say 'yes' to anything while she was paralyzed by fear."

Carlos was starting to get it. "I can see that."

Rick continued to explain. "When I asked Larisa to help me simplify the brochure, she quickly gained confidence by hearing herself repeat the features of the product on her own. So we were able to get to the source of Larisa's objections—her fear of being exposed as technically inadequate—and address those fears in the only way possible: by having her demonstrate to herself that she already knew enough to make a decision."

Carlos was nodding in agreement.

Rick added, "So this is part of a complete way of thinking about selling. And I've distilled these ideas down to just ten simple laws. Learn them, and I guarantee you will not only become a really successful salesperson, but you'll also love what you do."

Carlos could see that would be a better way to approach his job. "Can't wait."

Rick grinned at Carlos. "It just so happens that today you learned the seventh law, which is about learners and teachers, and you also learned the eighth law: Salespeople must address their customers' objections at the source of the objection."

"That sounds important," Carlos replied. "Would you mind repeating it so I can write it down?"

Carlos grabbed a piece of paper, and this is what he heard and wrote:

LAW #8:

SALESPEOPLE MUST ADDRESS THEIR CUSTOMERS' OBJECTIONS AT THE SOURCE OF THE OBJECTION.

In parting, Carlos said, "I'm beginning to get it. It's not about me! It really doesn't matter if customers buy because of me or not. The point is that they bought. Thank you very much for this."

"No problem," Rick replied. "I'm glad I was able to help."

They shook hands and parted ways.

Martin coached his next softball game that evening. Katya was pitching up another great game. He noticed Katya's Mom, Marnie, intently watching the game from the dugout. Martin decided to experiment with Rick's coaching principles. He began observing Marnie watch the game. Martin noticed how focused and genuinely enthusiastic she was about how the game was going. Based on his observations, her daughter Katya's performance and the team's success were obviously important to her. Martin also noticed that, unlike the other moms, whose focus was solely on their daughters, Marnie was interested in how the entire team was performing. Martin planned to strike up a conversation with Marnie about the team.

After the game was over and the Robins had scored another win, Martin immediately approached Marnie, before Katya came over. "Katya's pitching has been much better lately."

"It sure has," Marnie replied. "I saw a big turnaround after you brought that coach by."

"Have you noticed the team also seems to be playing better in general?" Martin asked.

"Yes, some of the girls are playing better, for sure. Others are still suffering from this season's doldrums, I'm afraid."

"You've done a good job supporting Katya through her tough time," Martin told her. "Is there any advice that you think her teammates would benefit from?"

Marnie was really delighted that Martin had shown an interest in hearing her opinion. "Huh...Thanks for asking! But I'll need some time to think about exactly what I want to share."

Martin took the opportunity. "Well, perhaps we can meet sometime so you can share your observations. And if you'd like, perhaps we could have you speak during a practice."

Marnie looked genuinely pleased at the thought. "We'll see. Maybe you won't agree with what I have to say."

Martin laughed that off. "I'm sure whatever you have to say will be valuable."

Katya came over to greet them, and then mother and daughter walked away, hand in hand.

Martin made a note to self: Marnie likes to hold hands.

Chapter 7

THIS TIME IT'S PERSONAL
Increasing Influence

Rick received a message from Sally. It said, "Hi, Rick.
I managed to get an appointment to meet with a supervising nurse
at Hope General. Her name is Zena. She's been playing hard to
get, so I suggested a lunch meeting, and she agreed to noon on
Monday. Can you meet me in the lobby at 11:45?"

On Monday, Rick met up with Sally in the Essentials' lobby.
Sally was soon driving and talking with both hands. Rick tight-
ened his seatbelt, just in case.

Sally said, "So Meg helped me out by giving me the contact
information for the senior training nurse, Zena."

"Did Zena express any reason for meeting with us, other
than a free lunch?" Rick asked.

"Not that I could ascertain. By the way, if you don't mind,
I'd like to take the lead on this appointment. I definitely want

your input on my presentation after we're done. But you know how it is—if I think you're about to jump in, it'll distract me."

Rick replied, "No problem. I know how that can be…"

"Thanks." Sally suddenly saw a car she thought was about to cut into her lane. She leaned on the horn and yelled in the car's general direction, "Hey, buddy!" Then, without missing a beat, she turned her attention back to Rick. "I've got to stop by Meg's. I want to thank her for Zena and also check on the tape inventory."

Rick's eyes were still wide, but he kept his cool and simply said, "Yes, checking in with Meg sounds like a good idea."

"By the way," Rick continued, "there's one thing I need to mention. Ben informed me about potential sales department policy changes going into effect because of cost-cutting."

"Oh?" Sally nervously replied.

"It may no longer be viable for our reps to visit customers as frequently as you have been doing," Rick explained.

"What will I do with the time I was spending to make visits?"

"You'll still be making just as many visits," Rick told her. "They'll just be to a larger number of customers. Repeated visits to the same customer won't be as frequent."

"Then how will I be able to maintain their business?" Sally asked. "If they don't see me as much, they might not feel as connected to us."

"I have an idea that might help," Rick replied. "Let's get into it later."

Rick and Sally arrived at Hope General Hospital. They walked over to Meg's desk, where she was busy at work. Sally loomed into view.

Meg must have been concentrating deeply on something when the shadow crossed her desk. She looked up. "Sally! And Rick! What a surprise. Look, guys, I wasn't expecting you, and I'm totally swamped."

Sally quickly interjected, "No problem. Actually, we came by to take Zena out to lunch. Thanks for your help."

"Oh, you're welcome," Meg responded. "Well, I do have a moment. Why don't I check the Bactogone tape and splint inventory while you're here."

Meg went over to her computer and said, "Nope—we don't need any more tape or splints. All the new Bactogone we received is still here. Maybe it's the cost thing. Well, anyway, good luck with Zena."

While they walked to Zena's office, Rick asked Sally, "Did you notice Meg completely forgot why our Bactogone tape is more expensive?"

"Yes, it's a little disappointing that none of the advantages sank in. I could have reminded her, but it wasn't the time for a big discussion."

"Agreed."

⬡

Zena looked to be in her late thirties, young for a head nurse. She was dressed in festive, patterned scrubs. "We've got to hurry," Zena told them. "I need to be back for a meeting in forty-five minutes."

"We can do it!" Sally assured her.

During their walk to the restaurant, Sally broke the ice by chatting about the traffic, discussing a new expansion the hospital was planning, and commenting on theories about why energy prices had changed so rapidly. Zena mentioned she had a daughter who attended the local elementary school. When they arrived at the restaurant, it was crowded and noisy. Luckily, Sally had a reservation, so everyone was quickly seated.

As they were looking at the menu, Sally asked Zena, "Are you familiar with my product? It's the Bactogone antiseptic splint and tape combination."

"Yes, Meg mentioned that she'd brought it in and that you might be contacting me. I did look up the price, and, frankly, it's the most expensive tape we have in the hospital. The penny-pinchers are breathing down our backs."

"You've got the product right," Sally responded, "but the price is actually the best value for tape in the hospital. Let me explain why…"

Just at that moment, the waiter came by. He asked what they wanted to drink, but Zena said they were in kind of a hurry. She asked Rick and Sally if it would be okay to place lunch orders now.

"Sure that's fine," Sally told her.

Once the waiter had left, Sally asked, "Since we don't have much time, would it be okay if I just jump into what I wanted to say?"

"Feel free."

Sally began her well-prepared spiel. She first went into the history of the manufacturer, producing data showing the growing concern about hospital-borne infections. Between bites, she described the splint and tape product in great detail. Zena seemed content to enjoy her lunch, offering Sally an occasional nod or an "um-hmm" during the spiel. Sally continued as if being cheered on by Zena's gestures. She covered the research behind the product, the concentrations of ingredients they used, and testimonials from satisfied customers. The waiter brought the check, and Sally handed him the company credit card. Rick wasn't sure if Sally was finished with her presentation, but it didn't seem to matter. Their lunch was clearly over as Zena stood up, anxious to make her next meeting. Rick and Sally picked up on Zena's cue and got up from the table to leave, too. It was a short, brisk walk back to the hospital. Zena thanked them both for lunch, shook their hands, and left.

On the ride back from the hospital to Essentials, Sally said to Rick, "I was able to cover everything I wanted to say in that short time."

"That's good to hear," Rick responded. "Do you think Zena's going to follow through on training nurses to use Bactogone?"

"I sure hope so," Sally replied. "She should, after everything I told her."

Rick said, "I hope so as well, but I really don't know if she will or not. Perhaps on Monday you can check with Meg on the inventory to see if the tape has moved at all over the weekend."

"That's a good idea. I'll give you a call on Monday and let you know what Meg says."

When Monday rolled around, Rick saw a message from Sally in his inbox. The message said, "Hi Rick. I checked in with Meg about the tape inventory. Would you please give me a call when you get a chance?"

Rick picked up the phone and called Sally. "Hi, Sally; it's Rick. I got your message."

"Hi, Rick," Sally responded. "I hope you had a nice weekend. I spoke with Meg this morning. Bactogone's still sitting on the shelves."

Rick said, "I have an idea. Let's talk to Meg again. I've got an appointment with a doctor at Hope General tomorrow. Since that's our regular rendezvous spot and it's on your way home, perhaps you could you join me after my appointment."

"Say when," Sally replied. "Just curious—what does your having a meeting with a doctor have to do with speaking to Meg?"

"I want Meg to know it's only a secondary reason for my being there."

Sally was puzzled. "Huh. Why would we want to downplay seeing Meg? Don't we want to show her that we're on it, that we care and follow up?"

"Actually," Rick said, "if Meg thought we were going to Hope tomorrow just to speak with her, I'm concerned our interaction with her would be too externalized."

"Externalized?"

"I think all interactions between people fall somewhere along a continuum of being external or internal," Rick went on.

Sally clearly didn't get it. "Okay…"

Rick clarified. "As you know, the point of selling is buying. This means we look at everything from the buyer's perspective. Anything that turns out to be about the salesperson will be external to the buyer. So if we blast in there just to see her, Meg's going to be defending herself and her space against our invasion. All of her feelings will be about us, about the externals going on at the moment. We don't want that, because her decision process is internal."

Sally began to understand. "I can see that. It's definitely in her space."

Rick nodded. "But we want the sales interactions to be internal to Meg. So ideally, we'd be moonwalking in the door—barely appearing to be going forward but somehow there. So instead of barging in, we were just passing by."

Sally replied, "Not being pests?"

Rick chuckled and said, "In so many words…yes. We don't want to tip the scale too much toward the external. That will result in her thinking our desire to contact her is more about something we want than about something she wants. If that happens, her behavior will become avoidant. That's a difficult situation to overcome, once it happens."

"All I've ever heard in sales training is how salespeople should take over interactions and get customers to think their way,"

Sally remarked. "I've never had a trainer tell me to get myself out of the way."

"If I were telling you what you've always heard," Rick said, "then I'd be wasting your time. I'm glad I can give you some new things to think about."

Tuesday at 11:30, Rick found Sally waiting for him in the hospital lobby. Rick motioned for Sally to have a seat so they could prep for the conversation with Meg. Then he said, "I'd like to use this meeting with Meg to make good on the promise I made to you. Today with Meg, I'll show you how to keep your sales up, in spite of looming restrictions on the frequency of your repeat visits."

"Okay," Sally responded.

Rick pulled a sealed envelope from his shirt pocket. He handed the envelope to Sally and said, "Don't open this yet. I've written a note that we'll read together after our talk with Meg is over."

"This sounds mysterious," Sally commented.

"Don't worry. It will all make sense in the end. What isn't mysterious is what I'd like to achieve today. I want to see if there's a way to get Meg to advocate for our Bactogone with the nurses. I'm not talking about just getting her to speak with the nurses. I'm talking about getting her to internalize the decision to do so."

"What would be the difference?" Sally asked. "Doesn't a decision to buy mean she'll speak to the nurses?"

"Not necessarily." Rick replied, "And while it may be possible to somehow cajole her into speaking with the nurses, that's not what we really want. We want Meg to be committed to making sure those nurses start using the tape. We want to know that she'll be taking initiative to do this without the need for us to intervene. That's what happens when she internalizes her decision."

"That sounds like a pretty tall order. Do you know how you're going to go about this?"

"No, not completely," Rick told her. "It wouldn't be possible to plan out the internal buying process that a customer will be going through. The very planning of it would mean that it wouldn't be internal for Meg. Customers need to have personal ownership of their decisions. That process takes place between the customer's ears. I won't have access to it. My job will be more of a supportive one. I think of it as more of a 'nonplan.'"

"So you're going to get all this accomplished by winging it?" Sally responded.

"Basically, yes. However, I can tell you in advance that I plan on not interfering with her internal buying process. I'm just going to let buying happen."

"That seems pretty obvious," Sally said. "What salesperson would want to interfere with Meg's buying?"

"Salesperson interference is more common than you think," Rick remarked. "My father was a farmer. One of the things he told me was that the potential for an entire farm exists inside just one seed. All that's required from the farmer is support in the way of soil, sun, and water. Everything else must come from the seed and time. The potential for Meg to be Bactogone's advocate is also inside of her. She needs to discover it and cultivate it."

"I understand it in theory," Sally said. "Now I'd like to actually see you implement it."

"Okay, let's go."

Rick and Sally walked over to Meg's desk. Meg was just getting back with a cup of coffee in her hand.

Rick said, "Hi Meg. I was visiting Dr. Ursaley upstairs, and since Hope General is our regular rendezvous spot, we thought we'd come by to say hello."

"Oh, hi," Meg responded. "You know Dr. Ursaley? He's a really nice guy, isn't he?"

"Yes, he sure is. I notice this hospital is full of great professionals. Must be a rewarding place to work."

"Thanks. It's true," Meg said. "One of the highlights of being a Hope General employee is the ability to work with so many good people. The outstanding doctors here make the medical benefits package they offer here even more valuable. I take full advantage of those benefits, because my son needs a minor procedure done here every month."

"Wow. Every month?" Rick exclaimed. "I know this is one of the best hospitals he could go to, but you must worry sometimes."

"I have to admit, I do worry about everything going okay. No one can be 100 percent certain of anything when you go into a hospital."

Rick took a careful gamble. "That's true; there's always a little nagging feeling of risk, isn't there? What do you think parents worry about the most when they bring a child here?"

Meg thought for a moment. "I would have to say the number one worry nowadays is hospital-borne infections."

That was bingo for Rick, but he showed nothing, said nothing, moved nothing.

Meg continued. "The chances of that happening are low, of course, but it does happen occasionally. The hospital trains all employees about taking precautions. Come to think of it, that's one of the reasons I bought your tape, Bactogone. By the way, how did the meeting with Zena go?"

"Hard to say," Rick answered. "Sally gave her a good explanation of why the tape will help Hope General reduce infections, but I can't say Zena was totally absorbing it. She was quite pressed for time."

Meg said to Rick and Sally, "It's frustrating that some important things seem to take so long before they are implemented here."

"What do you think causes the biggest delays here?" Rick inquired.

"I don't know," Meg said, "but Zena's having a nurses' meeting this week. I could drop in and see what goes on there. It's a good opportunity to let the staff know that in purchasing, we also have the patient's best interest at heart."

Rick asked her, "What points do you think would be most important to the nursing staff?"

"Well, I know they're concerned about contracting infections themselves," Meg said. "Bactogone would certainly help that. And Hope General's reputation is on the line. Patients will avoid our hospital if it's known for a high infection rate."

"Do you think they'll be using the new tape by the time your son comes in again?" Rick asked her.

Meg replied firmly, "It's going to happen."

On the way back, Sally remarked, "That was great, Rick! It went just according to plan—uh, I mean, nonplan," she finished with a chuckle.

"Actually, I hardly did anything at all," Rick told her.

"She came up with some great selling points," Sally said.

"Isn't that ideal?" Rick asked with a smile. "When your customer comes up with great reasons to buy, it simply doesn't get any better."

"As a salesperson," Sally said, "I've always been trained to be as proactive as possible. You're the first trainer to suggest otherwise."

Rick replied, "My father the farmer points out that, even though rice grows in water, you can't just toss the grains into a river. The momentum of the river's current prevents them from taking root."

Sally was wondering where this was going. "Uh-huh..."

But Rick knew where he was headed. "Meg's decision to advocate our tape to the nurses was like a rice grain. We took care to plant it in a suitable environment so it could take root. I made sure she knew I was there to see my doctor rather than primarily to see her. This prevented her thinking from building momentum before we broached the subject of the tape. If Meg thought we were making a special trip just to see her, she would presume it was about the tape. Her thought process would continue on. She'd think about how she has enough tape and doesn't need to talk with us. By the time we arrived, Meg's decision making would have built so much momentum that any mention of the tape would be met with stiff resistance."

After a moment, Rick went on. "Perhaps I compare plants to sales so often because I wish money grew on trees."

Sally remarked with a smile, "Thanks, Rick, for clearing that up."

She thought for a moment and then added, "Okay, I get your point. Hey—can I open the envelope you gave me?"

"Sure, open it up."

Sally opened the envelope Rick had given her earlier. It listed many of the benefits Meg came up with on her own: more effective for preventing infection, protect nurses and staff, already in stock.

Rick said, "All the selling points we wanted to cover were brought up, and she came up with more. The most important thing is that they came from her rather than from us."

They arrived back at the office.

Sally said, "This training was very cool. Okay, I see that it's possible to increase a customer's sales without having to visit them so much. I just have to keep that objective in mind during the presentation."

"Yes, that's right," Rick replied. "You have nothing to worry about with the policy changes. I'm available to help as well."

Martin's softball team was in the final inning with the Robins comfortably ahead. Martin glanced at Marnie from time to time, but she was intently focused on the game.

Marnie hadn't contacted Martin about her thoughts from their previous conversation. He had hoped she would have gotten back to him by now on how Katya's teammates could benefit from whatever had led to Katya's sudden improvement. Martin's typical approach would have been to approach Marnie and bring the subject up. He would have said something like, "I thought you were going to let me know what advice you'd like to tell the team." Instead, he decided to apply Rick's wisdom to the situation.

The fact was that Martin knew something was going to need to change when it came to dating. No one he had been interested in had turned out to be interested in him. The pattern was fairly consistent: Martin would meet a single lady he liked. He'd ask to get together with her for drinks or dinner. The first date or two would seem to be going okay, but then, when he'd call on a regular basis, the woman would start to avoid him. He could sense it each time it started happening. When he tried to give the woman more space, it always seemed that her mind was made up, and it just wasn't going to happen.

From listening to Rick, Martin began to sense that perhaps he was being too proactive. He thought about Rick's dad saying how a farmer can't pull on a plant to make it grow. Maybe developing reciprocal attraction was a natural process, just like buying. Maybe he was trying to pull on a plant that needed to grow at its own pace.

Maybe.

After the game was over, Martin approached Marnie. Martin decided that this time, he would leave behind any preconceived agendas. He'd just say hi and allow the conversation to go wherever it wanted to.

"Hi, Marnie. Pretty good game, don't you think?"

Marnie wasn't so sure. "I guess. But the other team made so many errors."

"No kidding. They played like they were under a lot of pressure. When Katya's on, like today, it's hard to get any runs off her…"

"That's true," Marnie replied. "And that really puts the pressure on Katya. She feels responsible for the whole team, like it's all on her shoulders." She turned and looked straight at Martin. "You know, she practices softball every chance she gets. I wish she were as motivated about school. She's got a big English project due next week, and she hasn't even started."

Martin wondered what he could do to help. "Do you think Katya would focus on schoolwork if she thought the team wasn't so dependent on her?"

"No question—but pitching is what she's great at."

Martin changed the subject slightly. "What's Katya's English project about?"

"She has to pick a quality that successful people possess and write about it. Her examples have to come from everyday experience."

A lightbulb went off in Martin's head. "Perhaps she'd be more interested if she related the project to softball."

Now Martin had Marnie's undivided attention.

"That sounds interesting. Like…"

Martin replied, "I dunno. Maybe she could write about teamwork. How one person can't take the burden for everyone."

"Hmmm."

"I know something about teamwork from my day job," Martin went on. "Maybe I could help."

"I'd really appreciate it," Marnie told him. "Why don't we all plan to get together, not just about her, and we'll just kinda sorta let her have this idea about teamwork."

"Saturday lunch?"

"Let's meet at Judy's Pizza," Marnie replied. "They've got a room in the back that's pretty quiet."

"Terrific. I'll see you two on Saturday at noon."

"Great!" Marnie responded. She gave him a big, warm smile as he left.

Martin thought to himself, "That couldn't have gone any better if I'd tried. Actually, it went better than if I had tried."

Chapter 8

I CAN'T HEAR MYSELF THINK
Selling To The Point's Three Cs for Successful Buying Decisions

Martin cornered Rick in the coffee room. "Rick, can we talk?"

"What's up?'

"Would it be possible for you to spend some time with Carlos again?"

"I think that can be arranged. What's the issue?"

"I'm sure you did all you could with Carlos within the time you had," Martin told him. "But I just think everything you said might not have sunk in yet."

"Symptoms?" Rick asked.

"Complaints from customers. They say he's still too pushy and assertive."

"We definitely need to nip that problem in the bud," Rick replied. "We can't afford negative comments on the web." He went on, "And another session with Carlos could help me test something I've been working on. I took you up on your suggestion at the softball game."

Martin had forgotten his suggestion. "Which was…?"

Rick wasn't surprised. "About selling. You suggested I get it down to a simple system so you could explain my training in your investor reports. I'd like to try my system out with Carlos."

"Sounds fine with me," Martin replied. "Can I sit in on your training with Carlos? That would make it possible for me to reinforce your suggestions afterward."

Rick suggested, "Perhaps the most effective approach would be for us to speak with him in the morning and then I'll go on a sales call with him in the afternoon."

Carlos and Martin were already seated and talking when Rick entered Martin's office Thursday morning. Rick got the sense that he had just walked in on a fairly intense conversation. Carlos seemed subdued, as if he had just been dressed down.

Rick tried to greet them as if nothing were going on. He turned to Carlos, saying, "I mentioned to Martin that I organized my sales training into a simple system."

Martin added, "When I heard that, I asked Rick if he'd be willing to go over it with you."

"Sure," Carlos replied. "What can it hurt?"

Carlos got up and walked over to the water cooler on the other side of Martin's office door. He still looked a bit shaken. He used the water break as a chance to collect himself. Both Rick and Martin noticed it would have been easier for Carlos to pour a glass from the pitcher sitting on Martin's desk.

After Carlos sat down again, Rick said to him, "I'd also like to join you on your 11:30 appointment today so we can try it out."

"I will do my best."

"Okay," Rick told him. "For Martin's benefit, I'll review a few things that occurred during our previous appointment with Larisa." Turning to Martin, he said, "Carlos gave an excellent presentation of the new model Q1016 thermometer. During the conversation, we discovered that new technology intimidates Larisa. She's also expected to justify her new product decisions to the engineers, which makes new technology intimidate her even more. The engineers like to ask 'gotcha' questions that make her feel inadequate. As a result, she shies away from purchasing any new electronics she doesn't fully understand. We got the sale only after she felt sufficiently confident about her understanding and her ability to explain it to the engineers."

Rick turned to Carlos and said, "What we observed was that Larisa came upon her confidence internally. In other words, we didn't need to convince her of it. She knew because she heard herself come up with technical product details. I know we already spoke about this after the sales call with her. I just want to set the context with you, because I have a new way of explaining it."

Carlos said, "Okay, I'm all ears."

"Let's use that glass of water in your hand as an example," Rick told him. "The amount of water you're going to drink is externally determined. It's determined by the amount of water your glass holds. If you drank from that pitcher of water on Martin's desk, which is more than you could finish, the amount of water you drank would be internally determined. It would be determined by when your thirst was quenched."

Carlos responded, "So far, so good."

Rick said, "We can look at Larisa's buying process the same way. Her confidence would have been externally derived, like the glass of water, if we suggested what she knew or needed to know. Instead, her confidence was internally derived, like the pitcher of water, because she stated the product details she already knew. When her self-confidence was satisfied, she made a decision to buy. It's just like ceasing to drink when the thirst is gone."

"Interesting," Carlos said, pondering it. "That's a good analogy. You taught me how decision making is an internal process on the ride back from our appointment."

"Yes, that's right," Rick replied. "What's new is that I worked out three simple requisites for good buying decisions."

"Three is good," Carlos said. "It might help me learn your method a little faster..." Carlos quickly glanced over to Martin and then turned his attention back to Rick.

"Great," Rick told him. "I call it the three Cs of buying decisions. Customers make the best buying decisions when they have the highest levels of these three Cs. Larisa bought because she had sufficient amounts of all three Cs by the end of our conversation. The three Cs are confidence, choice, and clarity."

Martin got out a pen and paper. He began taking notes on what Rick was saying.

Rick continued, "The first thing you need to know about these three Cs is that they're all internal. This is because decision making is internal. Therefore, a more accurate description of the three Cs would be internal confidence, internal choice, and internal clarity."

Martin wrote on his notepad:

> **LAW #9:**
> **CUSTOMERS MAKE THE BEST BUYING DECISIONS WHEN THEY HAVE THE HIGHEST LEVELS OF THE THREE Cs: INTERNAL CONFIDENCE, INTERNAL CHOICE, AND INTERNAL CLARITY.**

"I can see that Larisa gained confidence. Was it internal confidence or external confidence?" Carlos asked. "Is there a difference?"

"Yes—external confidence is the customer's confidence in the salesperson. But Larisa's internal confidence was her self-confidence as a decision maker."

Rick digressed for a moment. "You know, in old-school selling, salespeople will tell you that the first thing they try to do is earn their customers' confidence. So they're making external confidence their primary goal. How far is that going to get them?"

"I'm thinking it's only half the story," Carlos responded.

Rick confirmed his assumption. "Not even half. A sale can't happen without internal confidence. Customers who don't feel confident about their ability to make good buying decisions simply won't buy.

"By the same token, salespeople can't get customers to trust them without the customers first trusting themselves to decide whether they can trust their salesperson."

"Help me with something," Martin interjected. "Is there something wrong with customers buying because they trust their salesperson?"

"There's nothing wrong with it," Rick replied. "All the trust in the world is great. It would be wonderful if everybody could trust everybody else. It's just beside *the point.*"

Martin said quizzically, "The point?"

Rick smiled. "As in—the point of selling is buying. Good buying is an internal event for the buyer."

Martin could see it. "Aha."

Rick continued, "The 'uh-oh effect' comes from low self-confidence. So, Carlos, what was Larisa's uh-oh about?"

"Larisa's uh-oh was about being criticized by the engineers."

"Exactly!" Rick exclaimed. "That uh-oh disappeared when her intention was to tell us how the manuals could be improved. She was more relaxed, because suddenly we were the ones on the hot seat. I had reversed the roles. Her lack of understanding actually made her an expert in telling us how the manual could be better. And removing the uh-oh allowed her to relax and state more about the thermometers than she'd thought she could."

He asked Carlos, "What feeling did Larisa get in touch with when she gained confidence?"

"Her feeling of pride about speaking to the engineers about a new product?"

"Bingo!" Rick answered. "At the end of our conversation, she looked excited to be introducing something new to them. It was a good example of how internal confidence allows feelings to play a greater role in decision making."

Rick continued, "I'll talk about internal *choice* next, which is the second of my three Cs. Let's start by contrasting internal choice with external choice. A good example of external choice is salespeople trying to speak with the highest person on a company's organization chart."

"That's a basic law of selling," Martin interjected. "Everyone's supposed to do that."

Carlos added, "That's right, I've heard that in every sales training class I've ever gone to."

Rick said, "But think about it. The presumption is that whoever has the highest position in the company's organization chart will have the most choice. Right?"

Carlos and Martin both said in unison, "Yes, of course."

Rick went on, "Look, guys—in reality, that isn't always the case. During a conversation with the highest-ranking executive, you may find out the executive feels very limited about his or her ability to make choices. The executive may feel unable to choose because of limitations imposed by the board, unhappy shareholders, or restrictive regulations. A high-ranking executive may have lots of external choice yet lack in internal choice. Lack of internal choice is a major obstacle to buying."

Rick asked Carlos, "Okay, based on what I said, was internal choice a factor during our meeting with Larisa?"

Carlos answered, "It probably was. She didn't see buying the Q1016s as a choice until her uh-oh went away."

Rick agreed. "The biggest interference to internal choice is self-limiting beliefs. Larisa's self-limiting belief was that she could purchase only the products she could explain to the engineers. This belief greatly limited her ability to choose a new thermometer—even if she thought it was clearly a better one."

"Hmmm. That's interesting," Martin interjected. "I imagine that belief of hers creates self-imposed limitations on other buying decisions as well."

Carlos looked at Rick and asked, "Perhaps she'll enjoy benefits from our visit when she's buying other products as well?"

"I would think so," Rick said. "Perhaps she sees now that by trying so hard to avoid criticism, she could miss out on some good opportunities. In my opinion, one of the greatest gifts salespeople can offer to their customers is assistance with decision making itself. A big part of our contribution, as salespeople, is to remove interference to good decision making, such as self-doubts and self-limiting beliefs."

"I hadn't looked at the profession of selling that way before," Carlos responded. "This internal stuff makes my job seem a lot more gratifying. How would I spot customers who didn't believe they had many choices?"

Rick was quick to reply. "Good question. A telltale sign of customers with low choice is that they like and want the product but won't buy it. This can be a salesperson's most frustrating type of customer. We can't understand why the customer won't buy a product when he or she agrees it's a good product and well suited for him or her. Salespeople end up wasting a lot of time and effort trying to persuade these customers to buy. These salespeople don't understand what a critical role internal choice plays in decision making."

Carlos was running through a lot of history. "Wow."

Martin asked Rick, "How does that relate to the 'choice close' technique I hear about from salespeople?"

Carlos added, "I remember the choice close from selling school. They tell you to make decisions sound more like choices. Instead of asking, 'Do you want to buy this today?' I was trained to make it sound like a choice by saying, 'Do you want to buy the regular size or the economy size today?' Is that a real choice?"

"The choice close technique definitely relates to what I've been saying about the importance of choice," Rick affirmed. "Customers have a natural attraction to decisions that provide more choice and will avoid making decisions that result in reduced choices."

"Wait a minute," Martin said. "I'm not so sure about that. I've watched customers act the opposite way, putting off making a decision indefinitely because they had too much choice. They'll just go in circles."

Rick replied, "Excellent point and a perfect lead-in to the final C, which is internal *clarity*. All the three Cs support each other. Internal clarity supports internal choice for motivating customers. I'll first explain what internal clarity is by contrasting it with external clarity. Some good examples of external clarity are product features and product specifications. These are extremely useful tools for describing details of products to customers. Another example of external clarity is terms of purchase and delivery. Customers need to be clear about what to expect upon a product's purchase."

Martin replied, "All those things seem very essential to me."

"Yes, agreed. External clarity is definitely important. However, it's no substitute for internal clarity."

Rick went up to the whiteboard and started writing: "What the decision to buy represents to the customer." He explained, "That's my definition of internal clarity: when the customer understands the value and importance of her decision to buy. For example, if a tennis racquet customer wants to be the club tennis champ, then buying a tennis racquet represents taking a step toward being club champ. All the feelings associated with being club champ, such as achievement and satisfaction, will also be associated with purchasing a racquet. When customers are aware of what the buying decision represents to them, they have internal clarity."

"So," Carlos replied, "you're saying the tennis racquet customer has internal clarity if he's aware of the achievement and satisfaction he'll feel by having a racquet that helps him win the club championship."

"Yes, that's right. He's motivated, and buying the racquet represents a step along an important path."

"I noticed your buying proposition to Larisa was about justifying the decision to management," Carlos mused aloud.

"That's exactly right. My buying proposition, or close, was about her internal clarity. It wasn't about the Q1016 thermometer itself. I closed her on being able to justify a technical product purchase to management. Larisa brought up an additional point of clarity on her own. She brought up how pleased the engineers will be with getting the newest model electronic product."

Carlos looked at Martin and said, "Yes, the entire meeting changed when Larisa got in touch with her nervous feelings of facing management and the engineers. It was incredible!"

"Yes, that's right," Rick affirmed. "Simply discussing the external clarity about the thermometer's technical superiority and good pricing wasn't going to lead her to a buying decision. I needed to find out about her underlying self-doubts. The doubts were dispelled when she gained clarity about her actual ability to convey the thermometer's technical features. Once that happened, she could get in touch with the pride she'd feel from explaining it to the engineers."

Carlos asked, "If self-doubt interferes with confidence, and self-limiting beliefs interfere with choice, what interferes with clarity?"

Martin was pleased that Carlos asked such a good question.

Rick replied, "Lack of self-awareness prevents internal clarity. Customers lack clarity when they don't know what buying the product will mean to them. In other words, customers have to know which wants and needs the product will satisfy for them.

The key words are 'for them.' The same product could satisfy different needs for different customers. It's nice if salespeople know what the needs are for other people, but in order for customers to buy, it's essential for them to know their own needs. If a customer doesn't know his or her own needs, then how can that customer determine whether the salesperson's product will satisfy those needs? That's the essence of internal clarity."

"What are some common obstacles you have encountered to customers gaining internal clarity?" Carlos asked.

"Customers won't know what a product's features mean for them if they can't relate them to existing needs. Customers are more likely to be clear about their needs if they're clear about their goals."

"No strategy, no goals, no clarity," Martin observed.

Rick nodded in agreement. "Have you ever noticed how difficult it is to sell something to someone who isn't clear about what he's trying to accomplish?"

"It's like banging your head against the wall," Carlos replied.

Martin chuckled and said, "I've dealt with employees over the years who fit this description."

"Another type of customer with obstacles to internal clarity is the distracted customer," Rick went on. "I'd be here all day trying to name all the things that could potentially distract a customer from clarity. For example, the self-doubt that interferes with internal confidence and the self-limiting beliefs that interfere with internal choice are both distractions. These thoughts will distract customers' attention away from goals, wants, and needs.

Suffice it to say that if a customer is out of touch with his wants and needs, he is probably distracted by something."

Martin was impressed with his nephew's focus and engagement with Rick. He smiled broadly when Carlos asked, "How do you suggest I get a distracted customer's attention?"

"The first thing is to remember that whatever the distraction is, it's ultimately irrelevant to the buying decision," Rick told him. "When a customer is paying attention to goals, wants and needs, the distraction goes away—no matter what it was. Also, it's more important for the customer to be paying attention to himself or herself rather than paying attention to the salesperson. Customers must get in touch with their goals, wants, and needs. An overbearing salesperson can be as much of a distraction for that as anything else."

"Then how do I decide what to get customers to pay attention to?" Carlos asked.

"I find that a customer's feelings make an excellent source of internal clarity. I mentioned before that every decision is ultimately based upon an underlying feeling. Once customers get in touch with how it will feel to have the product, they get clear about its value."

"What feelings did Larisa get access to during our visit?" Carlos questioned.

"Pride," Rick responded. "That's what she felt when she could explain the Q1016. We didn't get the sale because of the thermometer's new features. We got the sale because of what those features represented to Larisa."

"Just because someone has lots of choices doesn't mean she'll make a decision," Martin put in. "Actually, just the opposite may be true. For example, some rich kids aren't motivated because they already have everything."

Rick said, "Yes, that's very true. Choice alone wouldn't have motivated Larisa—clarity was also required. Clarity took the form of pride in the fulfilling of her job description. Once she got in touch with her feelings, she became motivated to satisfy them by buying. This is how clarity worked together with choice."

Martin was impressed with how relaxed and focused Rick was, even while knowing his job was on the line at Essentials. He was coming up with these pearls, creating as he went along.

As Carlos was driving Rick to the appointment, Rick asked him, "What can you tell me about the customer we're going to see?"

"This is a catalog distribution company," Carlos replied. "The purchaser we'll be talking to is Anton. He's relatively new. Some of our thermometers are already in the company's catalog, but the sales with us have slowed down. The new Q1016 thermometer could be just the thing to turn things around."

They arrived at the appointment. Before they got out of the car, Carlos turned to Rick and said, "If you don't mind, let me start the conversation. He knows me, and I set up the appointment. You can take over as soon as you think you can help."

Rick smiled. "Sure thing."

They got out of the car and headed for Anton's office. Carlos regained the bounce in his step once he got away from Uncle Martin. Once again, Carlos walked several steps ahead of Rick. The office was in a red brick building that looked like it had previously been a school, and a warehouse with trucks parked behind it appeared to have once been the school gymnasium.

Anton opened the door, and Rick made some notes on him: shorter than both Rick and Carlos, tightly cropped hair. Black blazer, sharply pressed slacks, white shirt, and a thin, black necktie that was a little too tightly tied.

Carlos jumped right in by saying, "Thanks, Anton, for agreeing to see us today. Rick here is our company sales guru, so look out."

Anton said, "Pleased to meet you, Rick," as he shook Rick's hand.

Carlos continued, "I was looking at your sales history. It looks like we need to generate a little excitement in your catalog's thermometer section."

Anton cautiously replied, "Okay."

Carlos continued, "Essentials just released the new Q1016 model thermometer. It can withstand any type of sterilization without losing accuracy, and it has twice the lifespan of your catalog's current model—the P829."

Anton sat down by his desk and opened his laptop. He appeared calm and interested, typing the specs as Carlos continued to talk about the Q1016. Eventually, he said, "Sounds interesting. What are the price points?"

Carlos replied, "Right now you're paying $24.99 per unit for the P829. I can get you six cases of the Q1016 for just $29.99 per unit."

Anton peered up over his laptop at Carlos and replied, "That sounds good. I'm fairly new here, so management still reviews my orders before I can place them. I'll pass the information over to management and let you know what they decide."

Carlos glanced over at Rick, who knew this was his cue to jump in.

Rick remarked to Anton, "You seem to have a good command of the purchasing position for being so new."

Anton humbly replied, "Thanks, but I don't know if I'm so new anymore. I'll have my one-year anniversary working here by the end of next month."

"How will management know when it's time to streamline purchasing by letting you place orders directly?" Rick inquired.

"I'm not sure when that would be. Just whenever they decide to change it, I guess."

Rick continued, "The reason I'm asking is that you'd obviously be more valuable to management if you could take purchasing decisions off their hands. It would allow them to focus on other things. I'm wondering—if they decide every purchase for you, how will they know you're ready?"

Anton loosened his tie, "That's a good question. I really don't know."

Rick asked, "Have you ever tried just placing an order on your own to see if anyone had a problem with it?"

Anton looked a little concerned and sat back in his chair, folding his arms. "No, because I've always followed their guidelines."

Rick proposed an idea. "If you're willing to experiment, we can use a thermometer order to see if management will let you do some purchasing on your own. It'll show them your ability to place orders without their assistance."

Anton wasn't so sure. "Hmmm."

Rick continued gently, "Play along with me here. Now, if management were to suddenly let you decide to order the new thermometers, what would you base your purchasing decision on?"

Anton replied, "Well, the first thing I'd do is look at the sales history report to see the previous rate of thermometer sales."

"Just for argument's sake," Rick told him, "let's say you aren't able to access the sales history report. Is there anything else you would base your decision on? The reason I'm asking this is that management must think there are other factors you need to consider besides sales history. I'm surmising that if sales history were the only important factor, you'd be doing your own purchasing already. After all, you have the same access to sales history data as they have."

Anton replied, "Hmmm. Good point! The next thing I'd do is check with Devorah. She runs our order desk. She has a bird's-eye view of what customers are asking for."

Rick suggested, "Well then, would you be willing to call Devorah and run the order by her? Carlos and I have time. We can wait."

"Sure, I could do that."

"One last question before you call," Rick said. "What is your gut estimate of the turnaround time for six cases?"

Anton said, "My gut sense would be four months."

"Now let's see what Devorah says," Rick told him.

"Okay."

He hit a button on the speakerphone and gave Devorah a call. Devorah seemed forthcoming and happy to help. She seemed to like the fact that someone was acknowledging the important information her position could reveal.

Devorah said, "The P829 thermometer's sales have steadily dropped off. That's not unusual; most products in our catalog do that, over time. It's because customers get excited when something's new. It makes sales increase at first because they want to try it. Initially, there will be approximately a twofold increase in sales. But then sales slowly taper off until something new comes around again to replace it. I think a new thermometer would be a good way to generate some excitement in that category."

Anton asked Devorah to hold on for a moment, and then he turned to Rick and said, "Based on what Devorah is saying, we'd sell six cases of the new thermometers this first quarter."

Anton went back to his phone call with Devorah and asked her, "Do you think we would sell all six cases?"

Devorah said, "I'll make sure we do. We'll mention it to customers and get it moving. Let's stay in touch. I'd much rather have someone I can talk to deciding order quantities than have management doing it."

Anton thanked her for the input and hung up.

Rick remarked to Anton, "Wow! You're a resourceful guy, deciding to pick Devorah's brain like that. She couldn't have been more helpful."

"Yes, thanks," Anton said. "Devorah's an underrated wealth of knowledge around here."

"Let's check Devorah's prediction against the sales history," Carlos suggested.

Rick was very pleased to hear Carlos come up with such a good idea.

Anton pulled up the sales history numbers and said, "Sure enough, these numbers accurately line up with Devorah's observations."

Rick proposed to Anton, "Let's experiment to see if we can get you more recognition and responsibility. You place an order today for six cases of the new Q1016 thermometers. Give management an FYI about the order. I'll delay submitting it for a few days, just in case management wants to modify it. I'll bet they let it go through when you explain your rationale. This will be a huge step toward increasing your responsibility and your value in the company, if all goes well. If not, we can always modify it."

Anton said, "Okay, I'm ready to test the system. I think it's time for them to know I'm ready to do my own purchasing. Let's start with an order for six cases of the Q1016s."

During the drive back to the office, Carlos asked Rick, "Did you think he was lacking in confidence, choice, or clarity?"

Rick answered, "Actually, the three Cs were all lacking. Anton's original objection indicated a lack of internal choice.

He believed he couldn't choose to place the order. He believed management insisted on doing that instead. By asking how management will know when he's ready to place orders directly, I used clarity to increase his choice. Next, I asked him if he has ever tried to place an order directly to see what would happen. That question posed the possibility that strict adherence to the policy could be another self-limiting belief. He lacked hard evidence that management wanted the policy strictly followed."

Carlos remarked, "I'd thought you would have said Anton's clarity would be about his feelings. For example, his desire to be valued by management."

Rick replied, "That's a good point, and you're absolutely right. Clarity can occur at different levels. Anton's getting in touch with the desire to be valued by management is another valid type of clarity. It's an even deeper level of clarity, in fact, because it's a feeling. This is why I linked placing the order with being more valuable."

He continued, "You may have noticed he didn't ask a lot of questions about the thermometers themselves. Internal clarity involves what buying the product represents to the customer. It doesn't need to involve the product itself. Ordering state-of-the-art thermometers represented recognition of Anton's value to the company."

Carlos said, "Okay, where does internal confidence fit in?"

"I brought internal confidence into Anton's decision making," Rick told him, "when I challenged him to decide an order without looking at the sales history report. I asked him to guess at how quickly they would sell. Next we got Devorah's prediction. I wanted Anton to gain confidence in his own ability to decide what to buy. Actually, you had the instinct to have him confirm everything at the end of our visit by checking the sales report against his gut feeling. Nice work! This allowed us to prevent the potential uh-oh that sometimes comes with added responsibility."

Carlos replied, "So Anton's confidence supported his choice and his clarity. The confidence supported choice by providing evidence about his ability to make good purchasing decisions, removing that potential uh-oh. Confidence supported clarity when the sales history report confirmed his ordering accuracy."

"Yes, that's exactly right."

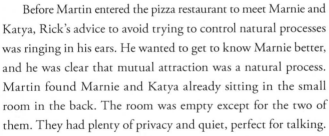

Before Martin entered the pizza restaurant to meet Marnie and Katya, Rick's advice to avoid trying to control natural processes was ringing in his ears. He wanted to get to know Marnie better, and he was clear that mutual attraction was a natural process. Martin found Marnie and Katya already sitting in the small room in the back. The room was empty except for the two of them. They had plenty of privacy and quiet, perfect for talking.

Marnie thanked Martin for agreeing to meet with them about Katya's school project. Then she said to Katya, "Why don't you explain to Martin what your project is about?"

Katya turned to Martin and said, "I'm supposed to pick a quality commonly found in successful people and write about it. I have to use examples from my everyday life."

"Do you have any ideas about what you'd like to write about?" Martin asked her.

"I think everyone's going to pick ambition or leadership, "Katya replied. "I want to do something different. I want to make it about softball."

Martin smiled and responded, "Perhaps you can. What quality do you think a successful softball player needs to possess?"

Katya blurted out, "A strong arm!"

Martin reminded himself that he was trying out Rick's approach. He held back the urge to propose an answer and said, "Yes, a strong arm is good. However, the softball player isn't successful unless she's on a winning team."

Katya thought for a moment and then offered, "What about good teamwork? Could I do my project on that?"

Martin exclaimed, "Katya, that's a great idea! Successful people need to have good teamwork, and playing for the Robins gives you a lot of experience with it."

Katya's eyes brightened. "Great," she said, "I'll make my topic about teamwork. And I don't think anyone else is doing that. Do you mind if I ask you a few questions about teamwork in jobs, since we have to include that?"

Martin smiled. "Fire away."

Marnie handed Katya a notepad and paper, saying, "Maybe you want to take notes."

"Fiona told me you're the boss where you work," Katya began. "She said your job is to tell everyone else what to do."

Martin cautiously answered, "Yes, it's true that I'm one of the bosses at work. But successful bosses understand they're not the only ones with good ideas. Sometimes they have to make a choice between reaching the goal and taking personal credit. If they ignore other people's ideas because they want personal credit, then they risk missing the goal. The goal is more likely to be achieved when everyone's ideas are valued."

"What about when the team relies on one key person to win? Isn't that leadership?"

"That's what I used to think," Martin told her, "but I've come to realize that if one person's performance is responsible for winning or losing, then there is a lack of good teamwork. That team member needs to put aside his or her pride and allow other team members to share responsibility."

Katya told him, "If this were about me, I would have less control over how the game goes."

"Successful people don't need to have control," Martin said. "They want to reach their goals. They know this involves relying on other people whom they can't control. This is okay as long as the entire team is aligned with the same goal and understands they'll reach it as a team rather than as individuals."

Katya thought for a moment. "That's what I felt when I worked with that pitching coach, Rick. Before I met him, I was trying to control my pitches so they would be like last season's pitches. He helped me see that my pitches were worse when I tried to control them. I needed to trust my arm to do the pitching.

123

I couldn't win games without the team of my arm and me. I know that sounds funny, but looking at things that way helped me improve."

"That doesn't sound funny at all," Martin told her. "It makes perfect sense. Do you think you can write a report on teamwork for your teacher now?"

"Yes, I can," Katya said.

Marnie was very impressed with Martin's thoughtful and attentive coaching of Katya. Both Katya and Marnie thanked Martin for his help as they left the restaurant. Marnie started thinking of ways she could spend more time with Martin. She liked how he was strong, but not bossy—a rare quality, she mused.

ONE LAST QUESTION
The Advantage of Using
Buying-Points over Selling Points

RICK'S MONDAY STARTED OFF WITH A BANG. HE HAD JUST pulled into his regular parking spot and was listening to the end of a news program when *bang*!—his car was jolted from behind. After recovering, he looked up in the rearview mirror to see Sally sitting behind the wheel in her car, covering her face in mock shame. After they had both looked for damage (there was none) and Sally had apologized for the fifth time ("Really! I thought I was already stopped"), they both headed toward the Essentials lobby.

Sally was excited. "It's so funny that I ran into you since I was about to drop in at your office."

"I think I prefer the 'drop in' as opposed to the 'run into,'" Rick joked.

"Really, are you okay?"

"Just teasing."

Sally rushed on. "Well, okay. So! I finally had a follow-up with Meg. And here's something strange. She wanted to tell me she'd figured out that the hospital's insurance premiums would go down 10 percent if they started using Bactogone."

Rick was confused. "So what's strange?"

"Well, I was disappointed because that was the selling point I was going to use. I had wanted to show her how smart I was," Sally explained. She waited for Rick to say something, but he didn't.

Sally then just blurted out, "Isn't that dumb? I mean, that's when I suddenly realized I've been prioritizing selling over buying. Everything else you told me fell into place after that."

Rick was pleased. "So you internalized the approach. The point."

Sally joined in. "Finally. The point of selling is buying. I got it."

"And therefore, how did things go with Meg?" Rick asked.

"Hope General is on board with using Bactogone. Meg got ahold of Zena last week, right before a nurses' meeting. All Meg said to Zena was, 'If your daughter were getting surgery here tomorrow, what splint and tape would you want to use?' Zena thought about it and said that 'for family,' she'd want to use Bactogone. Meg went with Zena to the training, and Zena took it upon herself to instruct all the nurses that Bactogone was it from now on. Bottom line—we got two huge reorders of tape from Meg just in the last three days!"

Rick exclaimed, "Superb, Sally. Congratulations!"

Rick was about to inform Sally about his discovery of the three Cs, but he sensed from Sally's suddenly raised eyebrow that she had a question.

Rick said, "Yes?"

"So...I have several appointments coming up," Sally said. "I understand your philosophy now, and I'm a believer. My challenge is figuring out how to integrate it. How can I state selling points anymore? Doesn't that just keep the whole thing about me?"

Rick paused. "That's a good question, and maybe we can answer it together. Tell me again what Meg said to Zena."

"Meg asked Zena whose splint and tape she would want the surgeon to use if her daughter were getting surgery."

A smile came over Rick's face. "Since the point of selling is buying, salespeople should rely on buying-points rather than on selling points."

"That sounds like something I need to remember," Sally told him. "Would you repeat it so I can write it down?"

Rick said it again: "Salespeople should rely on buying-points rather than on selling points."

LAW #10:

SALESPEOPLE SHOULD RELY ON BUYING-POINTS RATHER THAN ON SELLING POINTS. IT'S PREFERABLE THAT REASONS TO BUY COME FROM THE CUSTOMER.

"Meg was successful because she used buying-points with Zena."

Sally asked, "Okay, what's a buying-point?"

"A buying-point is something about a customer's situation the customer needs to be aware of in order to make a good buying decision. A salesperson can help customers make better buying decisions by pointing out buying-points in the form of a query."

"Would you please repeat that?" Sally asked. "It sounds important; I want to write it down."

Rick repeated, "**A buying-point is something about a customer's situation the customer needs to be aware of in order to make a good buying decision. Salespeople point out buying-points by asking about them. These questions are called buying-point queries.**"

Sally asked, "Did Meg somehow use a *buying-point query* with Zena?"

"Exactly," Rick replied. "Meg asked a question that got Zena in touch with her feelings as a mother and as a nurse as they relate to the splint and tape. The query was, 'What splint and tape would you use on your own daughter?' Meg didn't give her a buying-point, but instead helped her discover it for herself."

He continued, "So with regard to your original question, salespeople can use buying-point queries to improve the quality of their customer's decision making. And, importantly, the decision-making process itself will still remain internal to the buyer."

"Wow! I can't believe the answer is so simple!" Sally exclaimed. "Would you please repeat it so I can write it down?"

Rick repeated, "**The purpose of a buying-point query is for salespeople to improve the quality of their customer's**

buying decision while keeping the customer's decision making internal."

Rick checked his inbox and noticed a message from Martin: "I need to call a meeting with you and Ben re: changes to sales department policies in preparation for soliciting investors. Also, follow-up with Carlos would be good."

Rick ambled down the hall and looked in on Carlos.

Carlos said, "Hello, Rick, what's up?"

"I'm checking in to see how it's going with the three Cs."

"Well, actually, it's been a little rocky," Carlos told him. "They seem more difficult to use than I'd thought. I understand the theory, no problem, but it's difficult to think about the three Cs in the middle of a sales conversation. It distracts me, and I don't listen to customers as well. I suspect things will get easier to integrate if I keep practicing."

Rick replied, "Maybe this will help..."

"Okay..."

Rick continued, "Sally and I just came up with a way to get the three Cs working automatically. Since the point of selling is buying, you should rely on buying-points rather than on selling points. If you can find the right buying-points, the three Cs will be working for you."

"What's a buying-point?"

Rick went on to explain buying-points. He described how salespeople can pose buying-point queries to effect better buying decisions and keep decision making internal.

"Okay, let's see if I get it," Carlos said. "The buying-point we used with Larisa was her understanding of the new thermometer's benefits. The buying-point query was, 'What types of things in the manual did she think were confusing?'"

Rick exclaimed, "Yes, exactly! To devise a good buying-point, it helped for me to observe which of the three Cs Larisa was lacking. She lacked internal confidence. She wouldn't buy without confidence in her ability to convey technical information. As a result, I devised a buying-point query that showed her what technical information she really could convey."

"The buying-point with Anton related to his authority to make his own purchasing decisions," Carlos added. "The query we used was, 'How will management know when it's time for you to make purchasing decisions on your own?'"

"You got it," Rick affirmed. "Each selling conversation was oriented around the buying-point. The buying-point became apparent as we were talking and listening to our customers. From the standpoint of the three Cs, I noticed Anton lacked internal choice. Lack of internal choice was caused by a self-limiting belief that he couldn't make his own purchasing orders. Noticing this, I devised a query to question that belief.

"Once a salesperson discovers his or her customer's buying-point, the rest of the selling conversation falls into place."

Carlos asked, "You're saying I should pose buying-point queries rather than present selling points?"

"Buying-point queries should be the first tool in your toolkit to get customers in touch with their needs," Rick told him. "That way, customers can come up with their own reasons to buy. For example, on her own, Larisa recognized how excited the engineers will be to get a new gadget. The internalized rationales customers create will obviously be more convincing than any selling points salespeople could offer."

Carlos wondered, "But what if the customer doesn't say what he's thinking?"

Rick agreed this could happen. "The customer's buying process is internal, so it's possible you'll never know the insights and reasons to buy that the buying-point query created in your customer's mind. That's okay. The customer's buying process may remain internal. When that's the case, selling points are unnecessary. A customer may decide to buy solely because of what your buying-point query revealed about the decision. That's why buying-points are more important than selling points."

"Then would I still need to close?" Carlos asked.

"Sure," Rick responded. "Customers will still need you. Salespeople are their customers' stewards for turning decisions into action. Customers won't gain from their decision unless it's acted upon. For example, there are lots of people with good ideas for inventions, but only those who act upon their idea can benefit from it. By closing, salespeople invite customers to act on their decision and help them through the process."

Carlos was thinking hard. "That makes perfect sense. I'll tell you something. I've begun to stop thinking about myself all the time when it comes to selling. I've actually begun to think much more about our buyers and what they need. It's a big change."

Rick was pleased. "You're on the right track."

"Thanks, Rick," Carlos replied. "I really think I understand it this time."

━━━▼━━━

Rick made his way to Martin's office, running into Ben on the way, so they arrived together. Martin, however, looked a little cranked up, as in one pot of coffee too many.

Martin began the meeting by saying, "I'll get right to the point, gentlemen. I called this meeting because Joan will be back from her trip tomorrow. The first things she'll talk with me about are expenses I'm trimming from the sales department. This includes the salespeople's travel expenses. It also includes Rick's salary."

Ben overreacted. "Rick is not expendable, Martin! He's the reason Essentials has grown for fourteen straight years!"

"Ben, I'm on your side," Martin replied. "That's why we're here. We need to figure out a way to convince Joan that letting Rick go would be disastrous."

Martin turned to Rick and said, "You look unusually relaxed about this."

Rick replied, "That's because I don't see convincing Joan as very difficult."

Martin wasn't so sure. "Look, Rick, I've been talking to Joan, and she hasn't let up on this issue since it was first broached. She's nervous about how the financial reports will look to the board and to potential investors. She won't go along with anything she thinks is a gamble."

"That's fine," Rick replied. "In the meantime, I believe we've been developing one of the most powerful selling tools anyone's ever seen, and I think we can use it right here, right now, with Joan."

"Is that what you spoke with Carlos about yesterday?" Martin asked. "He called me this morning very excited about your conversation."

"Yes. Buying-point queries. All we need to do is find the right ones for Joan."

Martin was, to put it mildly, incredulous. "You're okay betting your career on this?"

Rick seemed content to do so. "As a matter of fact, I am."

Martin was surprised to find Joan's office door open. He walked right in and had a seat in his usual chair. "Welcome back. How was your trip?"

Joan did look tanned and relaxed. "I had a great time, thanks. I think I'm ready for the road ahead. How has your project been going with the department reports for investors?"

"Moving right along," Martin responded. "I started with the sales department, of course. As I was crunching the numbers, I came upon something interesting."

"Oh?"

"I presume you and the board wouldn't want to sell a majority of Essentials' shares to investors."

"No, of course not," Joan answered. "We want to maintain control of the company."

"How much control of the company would you like to retain?"

"Obviously, as much as possible."

Martin pondered her response. "Do you and the board have a range in mind for the percentage of shares you'll be selling?"

"Actually, you're touching a very sensitive subject," Joan told him. "Most of the board members are willing to sell up to 49 percent. A couple of other members, including me, would prefer to not sell more than 30 percent. At 30 and under, we retain the right to sell shares to family."

"So you want to preserve the option of keeping Essentials shares for your family?" Martin said.

"Yes. My daughters may want to work here someday, and I want to keep that option open."

"So the reason you want to get top dollar per share isn't to bring in the most revenue. It's to minimize the percentage of shares owned by investors," Martin remarked.

Joan said, "Yes, that's right."

Martin went on, "Then what we really want from these department reports is revenue, not necessarily investors."

"Okay," Joan replied, "you can look at it that way. Yes."

"That being the case, we should be open to any and all potential scenarios to increase revenue—even if we think they might not be attractive to investors."

"Okay, you've got a point," Joan said. "If I had to choose between revenue and investors, I'd choose revenue."

"I thought that might be so. I have discovered two recent developments. How we decide to respond to them will surely affect revenue."

"What are they?" Joan inquired.

"The first is a customer service rating blog of local medical product distributors. The second is the sharp increase in travel expenses due to rising energy costs."

"They're somewhat related to each other," Joan told him. "They both involve the sales department, and they both involve our salespeople's customer service."

Martin nodded. "That's a good point, Joan. Do you think it would be possible to address both situations with one strategy?"

"That would involve our customers buying more and being happier with our service while we're reducing salesperson visits to them. Can you show me a plan that will accomplish that?"

Martin reached down to an envelope that was resting next to his chair. "Try this."

He handed her the envelope over the desk. "Everything's a go. Sales will be reducing costs and increasing revenue."

"What are the bullets?" Joan asked him.

"I decreased fuel consumption by modifying the sales-people's routes. They won't be visiting each customer as often, which will drop costs significantly. Based on Rick's new research and training at our test customer, Hope Hospital, we've seen sales increase almost 200 percent with his new process. It takes some time to explain, but the short form is buying-points."

"I've never heard of a buying-point," Joan said. "Weren't we going to let Rick go?"

"Joan," Martin told her, "I firmly believe that without Rick to lead, train, and implement buying-points, sales are going to tank if we just cut travel."

"Hmmm," Joan replied. "I presume everything is detailed in the report you just gave me?"

"Yes, including the sales route modifications, buying-point explanation, and a balance sheet with the changes factored in. According to my new sales and cost projections, we may not need investors at all."

Joan replied, "That would be pretty darn wonderful. I guess I'd better tell Lila that Rick's not going to be available after all."

"We can't afford to lose him," Martin said.

<hr />

Martin's good mood lasted into the evening as he arrived for the final game of the Robins' regular season. The Robins had already secured their spot in the play-offs. The atmosphere was relaxed as the players and parents arrived for the game.

His daughter, Fiona, grabbed her glove and headed to the outfield. Martin decided to take a seat at the bleachers for a change. Being the coach, he usually preferred a more prominent place to sit, but today was different. He wanted to take it easy and see how the team played without his hovering.

He saw Marnie and Katya walking toward him. They sat down on the bleachers next to him, with Katya in the middle.

"Thanks, Coach," Katya said, "for helping with my report."

"No problem. I'm glad I could help," Martin replied.

Marnie looked over at Katya and said, "Go warm up now so your arm doesn't get sore."

"Okay, Mom." As she joined the rest of the girls on the field, Marnie thought it was very sweet how the girls greeted one another with big smiles. She noticed that Katya gave Fiona a warm hello.

Marnie looked over at Martin. "Is Fiona excited about being in the play-offs?"

"She hasn't said much about it this year," Martin told her. "Perhaps it's because she's still getting used to it. Or maybe she's just developing other social interests."

"Speaking of social interests, will Fiona be going to Emily's birthday-party sleepover this weekend?" Marnie asked. "Katya's looking forward to going."

"Yes. I'm forfeiting my weekend with Fiona for it."

"I guess if your time with Fiona is limited," Marnie responded, "it can feel like a forfeit. It's for sure a feeling of letting go for me. The girls are getting older. I guess it's inevitable that they'll be spreading their social wings more on the weekends."

She paused and looked into the future. "I guess my weekends are definitely feeling more spacious this year."

Martin sensed an opportunity. "Would you like to have dinner together on Saturday night?"

Marnie looked into his eyes and suddenly decided they were kind. "Sounds nice," she replied as she met his glance with a sweet smile.

A NOTE FROM THE AUTHOR

THE STORY DOESN'T END HERE—HOPEFULLY IT'S JUST BEGIN-ning. The true value of this book is derived from applying its principles. My job isn't complete until you experience success firsthand using the Selling To The Point system. The afterword that follows divides Selling To The Point's key principles into three sections: the ten laws, the three C's, and buying-point/buying-point queries.

The first section of the afterword lists Selling To The Point's ten laws. It includes explanations and examples to clarify the new perspective Selling To The Point offers.

The second section delves more deeply into the 3C's and how they relate to one another. Finally, in the third section, buying-points and buying-point queries are discussed so that you can begin skill building.

Afterword: Section One

THE TEN LAWS OF SELLING TO THE POINT

LAW #1: SALESPEOPLE WILL BE MORE SUCCESSFUL WHEN THEY UNDERSTAND THAT THE POINT OF SELLING ISN'T SELLING. THE POINT OF SELLING IS BUYING.

Law #1 sets the foundation for the entire Selling To The Point system. It reorients salespeople to where their priority really needs to be. Salespeople's success is determined more by their customers' buying performance than by their own selling performance. Those who focus on their selling performance are missing the point. The point of selling is about the customers' buying. This differs from traditional sales training philosophy, which focuses on the salesperson's selling performance.

Every sale involves two conversations taking place simultaneously. Traditional sales training pays attention to only one of those conversations: the selling conversation between salesperson and customer. It overlooks the second, more important conversation: the internal buying conversation that happens between the customer's ears. Selling To The Point is about salespeople working with their customers' internal buying conversations for more successful selling results.

LAW #2: A SALESPERSON'S JOB IS TO HELP HIS OR HER CUSTOMER MAKE A BETTER BUYING DECISION. SALESPEOPLE ARE DECISION COACHES.

Law #2 builds on Law #1. Salesperson success is primarily determined by customer buying performance, not salesperson selling performance. Customer buying performance is also known as decision making, which is a performance activity. It's similar to other performance activities such as sports and acting. Performers can benefit from having a good coach. The salesperson's role is to be the customer's decision coach.

If you're a customer, your reason for speaking with a salesperson is that you believe this salesperson will help you make a better decision. When salespeople share this goal, they work with customers as a team. Misunderstanding occurs when salespeople have a different goal than their customers have. The negative stigma people associate with the selling profession originated from a history of salespeople and customers not sharing a common goal.

LAW #3: DECISION MAKING IS AN INTERNAL PROCESS FOR THE BUYER AND SHOULD REMAIN THAT WAY.

Law #3 builds on Law #2. A salesperson's role is to be the customer's decision coach. While remaining on the sideline, a coach helps performers attain their highest potential. That way, performers can discover their inner potential while executing the task.

Unfortunately, many salespeople choose not to stay on the sideline. Instead, they try to exert as much influence as possible on their customer's decision. This interferes with the customer's attempt to make a good decision. Salespeople who steal the limelight distract the customer, diverting her attention from herself to the salesperson. It's preferable that a customer focus on herself while making decisions. If customers aren't aware of their internal wants and needs, they can't know how the salesperson's product will satisfy those wants and needs.

LAW #4: THE CUSTOMER'S DECISION-MAKING PERFORMANCE IS MORE IMPORTANT THAN THE SALESPERSON'S SELLING PERFORMANCE.

Law #4 may sound like common sense. However, think about the disproportionate amount of sales training time dedicated to improving the salesperson's performance rather than the customer's performance. It's a fact, however, that a salesperson won't get a sale unless the customer first decides the salesperson will be getting the sale.

Law #4 builds on Laws #3 and #2. The customer's decision-making process is internal. Decision making is a performance activity, and the most successful salespeople are those whose customer base consists of the best decision performers. These salespeople will successfully sell their product to everyone in their territory who needs it.

If a customer who needs the product doesn't buy, that customer didn't have a good decision performance. The interference preventing that customer from achieving his or her decision-making potential almost always comes from the customer. For example, the customer may have been basing his decision on a false belief. Another example is a customer with a false sense of urgency who rushes into a decision based on insufficient information.

The salesperson's actual role is to be the customer's decision coach. The coach is on the sideline, while the customer does the actual decision making. If the customer makes a bad decision, the improvement opportunity will be about the customer's decision process.

LAW #5: THE REAL TEST OF A SALESPERSON'S INFLUENCE IS DETERMINED BY THE CUSTOMER'S ACTIONS AFTER THE SALESPERSON LEAVES.

Law #5 builds on Laws #4 and #3. When salespeople encourage internal decision making, the decision endures beyond the salesperson's visit. Usually, a salesperson's success depends on how customers behave after the salesperson leaves. Salespeople must rely on customers to take initiative on their own. Customer initiative may involve using the product, reordering the product, referring the product to others, and staying loyal when approached by competitors. None of these actions will take place with the salesperson present.

A headstrong salesperson may find it easy to cajole customers into buying his product, but the real skill involves integrating that buying decision into the customer's personal beliefs and values. The true test of a salesperson's influence is whether customers internalize their decision.

LAW #6: THE LESS A SALESPERSON'S PERSUASION WAS INVOLVED IN A BUYING DECISION, THE MORE INTERNALIZED THAT CUSTOMER'S BUYING DECISION WILL BE.

Law #6 builds on Law #5. Customers are more likely to internalize decisions that involve maximum customer participation and minimum salesperson persuasion. Salespeople benefit when customers internalize their decisions to buy. An internalized decision occurs when customers not only buy but also buy in. Can you recall an instance when you were so thoroughly sold on a product that even the salesperson who sold it to you couldn't talk you out of it later?

Internalized buying decisions require the primary relationship to be between customer and product rather than between customer and salesperson. Salespeople who try to exert their influence don't give customers a chance to explore their own internal reasons for buying. The result is a buying decision that is salesperson-dependent.

Salesperson-dependent decisions are less desirable than internalized buying decisions. With the former, when the salesperson leaves, the customer's enthusiasm for the product leaves with him. This is why salespeople need to frequently revisit the same customers to maintain their performance numbers. Customers who internalize their decision to buy don't require frequent salesperson visits to maintain enthusiasm. Their enthusiasm comes from within.

LAW #7: IT'S BETTER FOR SALESPEOPLE TO BE LEARNERS THAN TO BE TEACHERS.

Law #7 builds on Laws #6 and #5. Salespeople should prefer that customers internalize their buying decisions. These salespeople understand that the most desirable scenario is for customers to think of reasons to buy on their own. Reasons to buy derived from a customer's own self-talk have instant influence. If a salesperson chooses to present selling points, it's important to select selling points that will integrate with the customer's beliefs and values. Doing this requires that salespeople first learn what those beliefs and values are.

Salespeople need to choose the selling points that their customers will be most receptive to hearing about. They do this by learning about their customers' interests. The best-devised selling points are worthless when presented to unreceptive customers.

LAW #8: SALESPEOPLE MUST ADDRESS THEIR CUSTOMERS' OBJECTIONS AT THE SOURCE OF THE OBJECTION.

Customer objections can originate from the customer's internal or external level. Salespeople must determine from which level an objection originated so they can handle it on the same level. Objections originating from the internal level involve customers' thoughts and feelings about themselves, whereas objections originating from the external level involve the thoughts and feelings customers have that aren't about themselves. Example: a customer says, "I can see how your product would help my business, but I need to be confident I'll get enough clients to pay for it." The customer's objection may be more about her confidence about obtaining clients than about the product's value. She's sold on the product, but she isn't sold on her own ability. As a result, she won't buy. Her objection originates internally, from self-doubts. A salesperson would not successfully handle her objection by addressing it on the external level. It would be ineffective to present additional selling points, exhibit more enthusiasm, or be more insistent, because the customer's objection comes from within. The salesperson would have greater success handling it on the internal level, helping her see that she'll have an easy time getting more clients.

Salespeople frequently fail to detect when objections originate internally. It's human nature to interpret everything as being about us. Objections originating internally aren't about the salesperson. However, the internal level's influence on decision making can't be ignored. If an objection is raised from the internal level, then salespeople will be successful only by handling it on the same level.

LAW #9: CUSTOMERS MAKE THE BEST BUYING DECISIONS WHEN THEY HAVE THE HIGHEST LEVELS OF THE THREE Cs: INTERNAL CONFIDENCE, INTERNAL CHOICE, AND INTERNAL CLARITY.

Law #9 builds on the previous laws. A sale won't happen without the customer possessing sufficient amounts of the three Cs. The three Cs are internal because decision making is internal.

A salesperson won't get a sale without the customer first deciding that the salesperson will get the sale. This decision takes place internally.

Salespeople are decision coaches, and the three Cs are the qualities that coaches attempt to instill in their coachees for optimal performance. The salesperson wants to instill these three Cs in her customer to help that customer make the best buying decision.

When salespeople notice customers possessing qualities that interfere with the three Cs, they'll help customers eliminate the interference. The main interfering qualities are self-doubts, self-limiting beliefs, and lack of self-awareness. Customers, not the salesperson, are usually the source of this interference.

LAW #10: SALESPEOPLE SHOULD USE BUYING-POINTS MORE THAN SELLING POINTS. IT'S BEST THAT REASONS TO BUY COME FROM THE CUSTOMER.

A buying-point is anything about a customer's situation the customer needs to be aware of in order to make a good buying decision. Salespeople coach customers by directing them to a decision's buying-point(s).

Salespeople introduce a buying-point to customers in the form of a question. These questions are called buying-point queries. The purpose of posing buying-point queries is to direct customers' attention to buying-points.

The use of buying-points is a better method for getting a sale than the use of selling points. The former allows salespeople to influence customer decision making at the source: within the customer. They also allow salespeople to influence decision making while keeping the process internal for the customer. Customers are more likely to act on buying decisions determined internally.

Internally derived buying decisions are better-quality decisions and are more likely to get integrated into the customer's personal beliefs and values. Internalized decisions endure when salespeople are no longer present, while salesperson-influenced decisions fade after salespeople leave. An internalized decision is more likely to result in customers using the product, reordering the product, recommending the product, or telling competitors they're loyal to the product.

Internalized decisions lead to customers arriving at their own reasons to buy—many of which, perhaps, the salespeople haven't considered. When a buying decision integrates into a customer's beliefs and values, the customer creates a personal rationale for buying. Customer-derived reasons are always more compelling than salesperson-proposed reasons to buy. This is the case even if that same reason was proposed by the salesperson. Have you ever experienced making a suggestion to somebody who doesn't act on your recommendation until he thought the suggestion was his own idea?

Afterword: Section Two

HOW THE THREE C'S SUPPORT EACH OTHER

A UNIQUE ADVANTAGE OF THE SELLING TO THE POINT SYSTEM is its simplicity. The number of requisites for optimal customer decision making are reduced to just three: internal confidence, internal choice, and internal clarity. As a result, salespeople only need to notice and help customers overcome three interferences to those requisites: self-doubt, self-limiting beliefs, and lack of self-awareness.

The three C's don't act independently during the customer's decision process. Each one synergistically supports the two others. For example, if somebody were using a map to arrive at a destination, clarity would represent the "you are here" point on the map. Choice represents the desired destination point. Confidence is the traveler's assurance that the journey between the two points is within her ability. All three Cs need to be present for optimal decision making. If the customer lacks confidence in her ability to make the journey, then knowing where she is and where she wants to go is useless.

The next section specifically outlines how this happens. It begins with a chart, which is followed by examples to help you recognize the supportive role each C plays in the decision process.

	Choice	Confidence	Clarity
Choice	X	Dispels the uh-oh effect to increase choice	1. Container for choice 2. Increases choice by exposing assumptions and increasing motivation
Confidence	Competence in new areas	X	Clarity dispels doubt
Clarity	Clarity is owned if it was derived from the customer's choice	Clarity is of little benefit without confidence in what clarity revealed	X

I'll briefly explain each cell of the the above chart:

Internal confidence supports internal choice.

Confidence supports choice by dispelling the uh-oh effect, which limits customers' choices through self-limiting beliefs.

For example, a customer who feels he doesn't know much about sports may decide not to advertise his product at local sporting events. Such events would provide a lot of product promotional exposure for a good price with a good market. The customer, however, doesn't view the opportunity as a realistic choice. He is scared that his ignorance about sports will cause him to make bad decisions in this market. He feels restricted to advertising only in markets in which he's confident.

Internal confidence supports internal clarity.

The benefits of attaining clarity can be realized only if there's confidence in what the clarity reveals.

For example, if a blind man using a cane thinks the cane will bend every time it touches something, he won't be confident that the cane is revealing where obstacles are. He won't be able to use the cane to get anywhere.

If a customer isn't confident that his or her feelings are valid, the feelings won't aid in making decisions. For example, a customer may be considering a vacation because the stress at work is causing her to feel run down. If the customer isn't confident that her run-down feeling is her body's way of signaling she needs a break, she'll opt to double her anti-anxiety meds so she can work harder. Her body's natural feedback process will be of little benefit.

Internal choice supports internal confidence.

Choice is increased when self-limiting beliefs and assumptions are dispelled. Acting on the newly discovered options will increase personal experience, which leads to newfound confidence about one's ability to handle the new experiences.

Let's use an art dealer example to illustrate this. The customer discovered that buying fine art was possible when the art dealer revealed its investment value. The customer began buying fine art as a result and, over time, gained confidence in his ability to decide what fine art to buy. He would not have gained this confidence without the clarity that (1) buying art was within his budget, and (2) fine art increases in value over time.

Internal choice supports internal clarity.

Choice allows clarity to be personally owned. Clarity that isn't autonomously chosen won't be fully integrated into the customer's system of beliefs and values.

For example, housemates may incessantly urge another housemate to get property insurance. The housemate may yield to the peer pressure and take out a policy. When this housemate moves, he's no longer exposed to the constant badgering about property insurance. He lets the policy lapse because he never independently chose to have a policy.

Internal clarity supports internal choice.

Clarity is the container for choice. In other words, clarity defines limitations for choices. These limitations turn the motivation gained by choice into action. The action that takes place is a decision. For example, the insurance salesperson may make the customer aware that she has only until her next birthday to buy insurance at the lowest price. This time limit to make the decision motivates the customer into action.

Clarity increases choice by exposing self-limiting beliefs and assumptions. For example, a customer speaking with an insurance salesperson may think he doesn't have enough money to buy more insurance. The salesperson provides clarity by pointing out that the customer has cash value in another policy that can be used to buy more insurance. This clarity provides the customer with more choice.

Internal clarity supports internal confidence.

Clarity dispels decision-making doubt. For example, once a customer feels how cold it can get in Montana, she gains confidence that spending extra money on a warmer coat is a good decision.

Both internal choice and internal confidence support internal clarity.

Customers will have greater confidence in their clarity if they arrive at their perspective through maximum choice. For example, someone who is told that his cancer is unexpectedly gone will be more likely to replace his old car. He becomes more confident about acting on his desire to own a reliable car. His sudden increase in life expectancy provides more choice.

BUYING-POINTS AND BUYING-POINT QUERIES

THE ABILITY FOR SALESPEOPLE TO CREATE BUYING-POINTS and to pose effective buying-point queries are the most important skills the Selling To The Point system offers.

A buying-point is something about a customer's situation of which he needs to be aware in order to make a good buying decision. For example, a customer needs to be aware of the tasks he plans to use a product for, before deciding to buy it. When a salesperson talks to a customer about his intended use for a product, the salesperson can improve the customer's decision about which product to buy.

Buying-points differ from selling points because selling points are independent of the customer's situation. For example, a selling point for a smart phone could be that it has the most features. A customer's buying-point for the same smart phone could be about how it will help him access email on the road.

The difference is significant. If the customer is intimidated by technology, the smart phone's extra features could be confusing. He wouldn't use it. The selling point about more features interferes with the buying-point about using it to get emails. For this specific customer's situation, the selling point is a deterrent to buying.

The elegance of using buying-points is that all three C's can be increased with a single buying-point. At times, it can also be effective to use multiple buying-points.

BUYING-POINT QUERIES

Salespeople use questions when introducing buying-points to customers. These questions are called "buying-point queries."

Buying-points are introduced as questions because decision making is an internal process. Questions are the best way for salespeople to redirect conversations toward the internal. A well posed buying-point query can increase all three C's while allowing the customer's decision making to remain internal. Multiple buying-point queries may be posed during a selling conversation. However, it's best to pose them one at a time.

The ability to create buying-points and pose effective buying-point queries involves practice and know-how. Below are some recommendations that will help.

1. Make sure the buying-point is about something essential for making the decision at hand.

2. The buying-point query should be about something the customer can easily observe.

3. The buying-point query needs to be open-ended and innocuous. They shouldn't involve a right or wrong answer. Avoid posing buying-point queries that risk putting customers on the defensive.

4. Buying-point queries are most effective if they intrigue the customer. An intrigued state of mind is optimally receptive.

5. It's usually best to pose one buying-point query at a time.

ENJOY SELLING TO THE POINT

SELLING
TO THE POINT®

HOW TO CONTACT
THE AUTHOR

I am committed to helping readers integrate Selling To The Point's principles into their professional lives. I consult for organizations wanting to integrate a more conscious approach to selling into the company culture. To this end, I give keynote addresses introducing this new perspective on improving salesperson performance; I lead workshops to develop the skills outlined in this book; and I consult for individuals and companies desiring to customize Selling To The Point's principles for their specific needs.

I can be contacted at:

Email:	JeffL@sellingtothepoint.com
Website:	www.sellingtothepoint.com

Made in the USA
San Bernardino, CA
17 October 2016